TREN DE ARAGUA

When the Tren de Aragua appeared in American headlines in 2024, most of the world was encountering it for the first time. Rolnar Armando Sanabria Bernatte had known it years before — from inside the system that incubated it.

A former Chief Prosecutor in Venezuela's Public Ministry with over fifteen years pursuing organized crime, Sanabria Bernatte built this book from a vantage point no outside analyst can replicate: that of someone who knows the Venezuelan judicial system, the penitentiary system that produced the band, and the institutional codes that have protected its members from international justice for two decades.

TREN DE ARAGUA: Anatomy of a Transnational Criminal Empire is the definitive reference for understanding this organization: from its origins inside Tocorón prison to its documented presence in 46 American states, from the trafficking crimes destroying lives in Nashville and the Bronx to the narco-terrorism charges that led to Nicolas Maduro's capture on January 3, 2026.

This book is simultaneously rigorous criminology, applicable operational intelligence, and a concrete public policy proposal. The book's intended audience includes FBI agents confronting TdA in the field, federal prosecutors building RICO cases, legislators crafting policy, and any citizen who wants to understand one of the most complex security threats of our era.

"Deconstructing Transnational Criminal Networks: A Venezuelan Prosecutor's Perspective,"

109th International Conference · International Association for Identification · Orlando, Florida, 2025

RESEARCH PRESENTED TO THE INTERNATIONAL FORENSIC SCIENTIFIC COMMUNITY "Methodology for the Investigation of Transnational Criminal Threats"

4th International Forensic Congress · IAI Colombia Division · Medellín, Colombia, 2025

TREN DE ARAGUA

Anatomy of a Transnational Criminal Empire

Criminological and Criminalistic Analysis of Organized Crime That Defies Borders, Institutions, and Governments

Rolnar Armando Sanabria Bernatte

J.D. · LL.M. · Ph.D. in International Public Law
Former Prosecutor, Public Ministry of Venezuela
Executive Chairman, Latino Institute for Security Efficiency

Latino Institute for Security Efficiency (LISE)

CAGE: 157Z2 | UEI: XQ1ELJLHYBR9

Tulsa, Oklahoma | latinosecurity.com/en/

Published by the Latino Institute for Security Efficiency (LISE)

7633 E 63rd Pl, Suite 300, Tulsa, Oklahoma 74133-1202

United States of America

ISBN: 979-8-9956962-0-9 (print Spanish edition)

ISBN: 979-8-9956962-1-6 (Print English edition)

For permission requests, write to the author at:

info@latinoinstituteforsecurityefficiency.com

LEGAL DISCLAIMER: This book is based on documentary research, public judicial records, unsealed federal indictments, government agency reports, and the author's professional experience. The opinions expressed are solely those of the author and do not represent the official position of any government agency. Cases cited are in the public domain or have been duly referenced.

Printed in the United States of America

DEDICATION

To Yenny, my partner in life,

and to our children, Victoria and Armando,

Who push me to be better every day.

To the victims of the Tren de Aragua —

extorted women, terrorized families, exploited migrants —

whose stories are the reason this book exists.

And to all those who work tirelessly

so that justice is not a privilege.

TABLE OF CONTENTS

Dedication... VII

Table of Contents... IX

Preface... XV

Foreword (Dr. Dagoberto Hernández)..................... XVIII

Acknowledgments.. XX

About the Author... XXII

CHAPTERS

CHAPTER ONE... 24

What Is Transnational Organized Crime?................ 24

   Opening Note from the Author........................... 24

   Introduction: The Security Threat of Our Generation. 25

   I. Defining Transnational Organized Crime.............. 27

   II. Historical Evolution: From Local Gangs to Global
   Enterprises 35

   III. What Makes a Criminal Organization "Organized" 39

   IV. Theoretical Frameworks: How Scholars Explain
   Organized Crime 42

   V. The Transnational Dimension: Why Borders Are a
   Criminal Advantage 45

   VI. The Socioeconomic and Political Impact of
   Transnational Organized Crime............................. 48

   VII. Key Terms and Definitions for This Book........... 51

   VIII. Chapter Summary and Forward Look 53

CHAPTER TWO 55

Venezuela: The State That Incubated the Monster 55

   Author's Note: What Only a Venezuelan Prosecutor
   Can Say 55

I. Venezuela Before the Collapse: The State That Was 56

II. The Pranato System: How the State Lost Control of Its Own Prisons 59

III. From Prison Walls to the Streets: The First Expansion.. 64

IV. Transnationalization: Following the Diaspora....... 67

V. The Historic Reckoning: The Capture of Maduro, January 3, 2026... 71

VI. The New Landscape: Venezuela After the Capture 80

VII. Timeline: Venezuela, the Tren de Aragua, and the Institutional Collapse 85

VIII. Chapter Summary: What Venezuela's History Teaches 88

CHAPTER THREE.. 91

Anatomy of the Organization.................................. 91

Introductory Note: Why This Chapter Matters in the Field 91

I. The Organizational Model: The Criminal Franchise 92

II. The Organization's Lexicon: Field Reference Guide 96

III. The Criminal Portfolio: Diversification and Evolution 101

IV. Terror as Strategic Instrument: Digital Warfare.. 108

V. Member Identification: Correct Criteria and Common Errors 109

VI. The Expansion Model on American Soil 114

VII. Chapter Operational Summary 116

CHAPTER FOUR.. 123

Human Trafficking: The Invisible Crime 123

Warning and Purpose of This Chapter 123

I. Human Trafficking as a Strategic Pillar of TdA 124

II. The Trafficking Cycle: The Four Phases. 127

III. Specific Routes to the United States 136

IV. The Federal Legal Framework: Tools for
Prosecution 140

V. Key Federal Cases: What the Formal Indictments
Say 143

VI. The Victims: Who They Are and How to Help Them
.... 144

VII. Chapter Summary: What This Chapter Demands of
Professionals 148

CHAPTER FIVE 151

The Tren de Aragua in the United States 151

Introductory Note 151

I. The Documented Presence: What We Know with
Certainty 151

II. The Nino Guerrero Indictment: The Definitive
Charge (December 2025) 154

III. The Analytical Debate: A Calibrated Threat
Assessment 156

IV. The Information Gap: The Venezuelan Records
Problem 158

V. Summary: The Threat Landscape in 2026 159

CHAPTER SIX 161

The Financial Architecture of Crime............................ 161

Introductory Note: Why Money Matters 161

I. The TdA Economy: Revenue Sources and Scale 162

II. Money Laundering: Converting Crime into Wealth
.... 164

III. Financial Prosecution Tools 166

IV. Summary: The Follow-the-Money Strategy........ 168

CHAPTER SEVEN 170

International Legal Framework and Policy
Recommendations 170

Introductory Note: From Analysis to Action 170

I. The International Legal Framework: Available Tools
.... 171

II. Concrete Public Policy Recommendations.......... 173

III. The Latino Institute for Security Efficiency: The
Value Proposition 176

IV. Summary: An Action Agenda for 2026 178

CHAPTER EIGHT 180

The Regional and Global Response 180

Introductory Note: The Decisive Moment of the
International Response 180

I. The Wave of Terrorist Designations: An Emerging
Regional Consensus 180

II. Joint Operations: What Has Been Achieved........ 182

III. What We Learn from Successes and Failures ... 188

IV. The Future of the Response: Toward a Hemispheric
Security Architecture 190

V. Summary: The Battle Map in 2026..................... 192

CHAPTER NINE...193

The Forensics of Terror: 193

Crime Scene, Victims, and Evidence in Tren de Aragua
Cases. 193

I. The Crime Scene in TdA-Related Cases 193

II. Forensic Identification of TdA Victims 197

2.1 The Challenge: Victims Who Do Not Speak 197

III. Documented Cases — Forensic Methodology in Action 199

3.1 The Ojeda Case — When the Crime Scene Speaks for the System 199

IV. Chain of Custody: Venezuela vs. the United States 202

V. Technical Recommendations for Agents and Prosecutors 205

VI. Conclusion: The Evidence the Venezuelan System Cannot Provide.. 208

CHAPTER TEN 210

The Venezuelan Criminal Records Verification Program .210

Author's Note: The Chapter This Book Exists to Write 210

I. The Problem: The Information Gap Nobody Has Been Able to Close.. 211

II. The Venezuelan Criminal Records Verification Program (VCRVP).. 212

III. The LISE Differentiator: Why Only We Can Do This 216

IV. The Federal Business Case: Why Government Should Invest in the VCRVP 218

V. Immediate Recommendations: What Can Be Done Today 219

VI. Conclusion: One Book, One Proposal, One Window of Opportunity 221

Glossary of Key Terms 224

Bibliography and References 231

Appendix A: Complete Timeline 1999-2026 235

Appendix B: Organizations, Designations, and Legal Frameworks 237

Appendix C: Resources for Victims and First Responders 238

Appendix D: Contact and Services — Latino Institute for Security Efficiency 239

Preface

On January 3, 2026, in the early hours before dawn, U.S. special forces captured Nicolas Maduro in Caracas. That same day, the Southern District of New York unsealed an indictment naming, among the former Venezuelan president's co-defendants, the leader of the Tren de Aragua: Héctor Rusthenford Guerrero Flores, alias "Niño Guerrero." That moment — in which a head of state and the leader of a transnational criminal organization appeared in the same judicial document — represents, perhaps better than any other single fact, the confluence that this book attempts to explain.

I did not arrive at this topic through headlines. I arrived at it through case files, courtrooms, crime scenes, and years as a prosecutor in Venezuela's Public Ministry. I watched up close as the institutions that were supposed to protect Venezuelan citizens were hollowed out, one by one, of their capacity to fulfill that function. I watched as the penitentiary system — the very one that was supposed to contain and rehabilitate offenders — became an incubator for the most dangerous organized crime in the Western Hemisphere.

When I decided to write this book, I asked myself a question: what is still missing from the public and academic debate about the Tren de Aragua? The answer was clear. Missing is the perspective of the professional who knows the Venezuelan system from within — not as an outside observer, but as an institutional actor who lived its collapse in real time. Missing is the analysis that connects the band's prison origins to its current operational method on American soil. And missing, above all, is the concrete proposal for how to close the information gap that has allowed this organization to operate with relative impunity in the United States.

This book attempts to fill those voids.

It is not an easy book. It describes crimes that troubled my conscience during the years I spent researching them. Human trafficking — the cycle of deception, transport, control, and exploitation that the Tren de Aragua has perfected across two continents — is one of the most difficult subjects to document without losing sight of the humanity of the victims. I have tried to do so with rigor and respect. If at any point the analysis becomes technical and distant, I hope the reader understands that this distance is not indifference: it is the only way to study horror without being paralyzed by it.

This book has three simultaneous audiences, and each will find something different in it. Security professionals —

FBI, DEA, ICE agents, federal prosecutors, intelligence analysts — will find operational intelligence here: the band's lexicon, victim identification patterns, money laundering mechanisms, and the legal architecture available to prosecute the organization as a criminal enterprise. Legislators and policymakers will find concrete, evidence-based recommendations on how to respond to this threat with precision, avoiding the costly errors of mass identification without methodological foundation. And the public — the citizen, the neighbor, the journalist — will find the most complete available explanation of how a Venezuelan prison gang became the fastest-growing transnational criminal organization in the Western Hemisphere.

The book ends with a proposal: the Venezuelan Criminal Records Verification Program, developed by the Latino Institute for Security Efficiency. It is not a theoretical proposal. It is a concrete operational mechanism, grounded in my direct knowledge of the Venezuelan system, that can begin functioning within weeks if the institutional will exists to activate it. The window opened by Maduro's capture will not remain open indefinitely.

The time to act is now.

Rolnar Sanabria. *Tulsa, Oklahoma, 2026.*

FOREWORD

At this moment, as you read these lines, the Tren de Aragua operates in 46 states of the United States, in over 15 countries, and in communities that five years ago had never heard that name. This book explains how they got there — and how to stop them.

I met Dr. Rolnar Armando Sanabria Bernatte at the 109th International Conference of the IAI in Orlando, Florida, in August 2025, where he presented his research on deconstructing transnational criminal networks before the international forensic community. What I saw that day — the rigor, the methodology, the unique perspective of someone who had been inside the system that incubated this organization — motivated the formal invitation from IAI Colombia Division for him to bring his work to the IV International Forensic Congress in Medellín, three months later. It is not often that one finds someone who has been inside the system that incubated a criminal organization and who, in addition, has the academic preparation and the vocation to document it with forensic precision.

In a world where organized crime evolves faster than our institutions, this work contributes something scarce: the scientific method applied to a real and present threat. As experts in identification and forensic science, we know that what cannot be identified cannot be prosecuted or dismantled. Dr. Sanabria breaks down with precision what he calls the "Forensics of Terror" — offering the contemporary investigator tools for crime scene analysis, victim identification, criminal semiotics, and chain of custody protocols that are directly applicable to fieldwork.

Colombia has suffered firsthand the impact of the Tren de Aragua. This organization has challenged our borders, overwhelmed our justice systems, and undermined the security of our communities. Therefore, this book is not just an academic analysis — it is a necessary contribution to hemispheric security and an urgent call for international cooperation among law enforcement agencies. Only through intelligence exchange and the standardization of forensic protocols can we successfully face this global threat.

I wish this work the reach it deserves and the reception it needs — especially among those who bear the responsibility of investigating, prosecuting, and dismantling transnational organized crime.

Dr. Dagoberto Hernández Ramírez
President, IAI Colombia Division (2020–2024)
International Association for Identification
Colombia, 2026

Acknowledgments

This book would not have been possible without the confluence of many people, institutions, and experiences that have shaped my trajectory as a prosecutor, criminologist, and security consultant.

To my wife Yenny and my children Victoria and Armando, for their infinite patience during the months of research and writing, for the weekends surrendered to work, and for being the constant reminder of why it is worth fighting for a safer and more just society. To my mother, Olga, who taught me that knowledge is the only inheritance no one can ever take from you.

To my colleagues at Venezuela's Public Ministry — prosecutors, investigators, judicial officials — who for years exercised their duty with integrity in increasingly adverse circumstances. Their commitment to justice, despite everything, is an example this book tries to honor.

To the researchers, journalists, and academics whose rigorous work on the Tren de Aragua, Venezuelan organized crime, and hemispheric migration has built the knowledge on which this book rests: InSight Crime, the Secure Free Society Institute, the Human Rights Foundation, the U.S. Department of State, the Department of Justice, the Department of Homeland Security, and the federal prosecutors of the Southern District of New York who have built the most complete judicial record on this organization.

To the victims of the Tren de Aragua who have had the courage to speak, to testify, to not surrender to fear. Their testimonies are the reason for this work.

To the International Association for Identification and the IAI Colombia Division, for the honor of presenting my research at their international conferences and for their commitment to advancing forensic knowledge.

To all the agents, prosecutors, social workers, and first responders who work daily to identify TdA victims, prosecute its members, and protect vulnerable communities: this book is written for you.

ABOUT THE AUTHOR

Rolnar Armando Sanabria Bernatte, J.D. · LL.M. · Ph.D.

Rolnar Armando Sanabria Bernatte is Executive Chairman of the Latino Institute for Security Efficiency (LISE), a federal consulting organization registered on SAM.gov, CAGE: 157Z2, based in Tulsa, Oklahoma, specializing in Venezuelan criminal intelligence, transnational organized crime, and border security.

Academic Background

Post-Doctorate in International Criminal Law, Emerging Technologies and Education · Doctor of Philosophy in Human Rights (Ph.D.) Master of Laws in Criminal Law and Criminology (LL.M.) · Juris Doctor (J.D.) · Graduate Studies in Criminal Law · Advanced Studies in International Human Rights Law.

Academic credentials evaluated and certified as equivalent to the American university system by Morningside Evaluations and Consulting, New York — recognized by the U.S. Citizenship and Immigration Services (USCIS).

Professional Background

With eight years as a prosecutor at Venezuela's Public Ministry and over fifteen years of experience in the Venezuelan penal system, he processed thousands of complex criminal cases, including organized crime, human trafficking, drug trafficking, and white-collar crime. He worked directly within the Venezuelan prison system during the period in which the Tren de Aragua consolidated its institutional presence, providing him with unique, firsthand knowledge of the mechanisms that enabled the rise of this organization.

United Nations (OHCHR) Documented Source (2018)

In January 2018, the Office of the United Nations High Commissioner for Human Rights formally certified Dr. Sanabria Bernatte's role as an expert source of information for the United Nations comprehensive report on human rights, corruption, and impunity in Venezuela (UN Resolution A/HRC/39/L.1/Rev.1). His independent technical data was utilized specifically to document institutional collapse for the United Nations Human Rights Council sessions in Geneva

Academic & Research Activity

• Mentor — IALEIA Mentoring Program, International Association of Law Enforcement Intelligence Analysts, 2026

• Speaker — IV International Forensic Congress, IAI Colombia Division, Medellín, November 2025

• Research Presentation — 109th International Conference, International Association for Identification (IAI), Orlando, Florida, August 2025

• Publication in Revista Summa Ratio on transnational organized crime

• Crime prevention and public safety lecturer, over 10 years

CHAPTER ONE

What Is Transnational Organized Crime?

Definitions, Frameworks, and the New Threat Landscape

Opening Note from the Author

Before the first analysis, before the statistics, before the legal frameworks — there is a human reality. Every number in this book represents a person: a migrant extorted at a border crossing, a business owner threatened by the "vacuna," a woman trafficked across three countries in weeks. I have prosecuted thousands of such cases in Venezuela. I have seen what organized crime does to communities up close, in courtrooms, at crime scenes, and in the faces of victims who never expected that the promise of a better life would lead to a criminal network's exploitation.

This book is not written for criminals. It is written for those who confront them: law enforcement agents, federal investigators, security executives, legislators, and policymakers in the United States who face an organization — the Tren de Aragua — unlike any they have encountered before. My goal is to provide you with the intelligence, the legal tools, and the strategic understanding you need to act effectively.

I write with a perspective that is rare in the American security discourse: that of a former Chief Prosecutor of Venezuela's Public Ministry, a criminologist, an academic, and an immigrant who has lived inside both the system that produced the Tren de Aragua and the American institutions now tasked with combating it. That intersection is this book's singular analytical vantage point.

Introduction: The Security Threat of Our Generation

The post-Cold War international order was built on the assumption that the primary threats to global security were nation-state actors: rival governments, nuclear arsenals, and territorial disputes. What the architects of that order failed to anticipate was the rise of a new category of power — transnational organized crime — that operates outside state authority, exploits the very infrastructure of globalization, and inflicts damage that rivals armed conflict in scale and human cost.

In 2024, the United Nations Office on Drugs and Crime (UNODC) estimated that transnational organized crime generates approximately $2.2 trillion annually —

roughly the GDP of Italy — while undermining democratic institutions, fueling migration crises, and corrupting law enforcement in countries from South America to Europe to the United States. The modern criminal organization is not a gang of opportunistic thieves. It is a sophisticated enterprise with logistics networks, financial instruments, digital infrastructure, and adaptive operational doctrine that rivals legitimate corporations in complexity.

Among these organizations, one has risen with startling speed to become one of the most discussed, most feared, and least understood threats in the Western Hemisphere: the Tren de Aragua. Born inside a Venezuelan prison in the early 2000s, this criminal band has — in less than two decades — expanded to over fifteen countries, established a presence on American soil, and attracted the attention of the U.S. Department of Justice, the Department of Homeland Security, and the U.S. Congress.

Understanding the Tren de Aragua requires first understanding the broader phenomenon of which it is a part: transnational organized crime. This chapter provides the foundation. It defines the key terms, examines the international legal framework, traces the historical evolution of criminal organizations from local gangs to global enterprises, and identifies the structural features that distinguish a transnational criminal organization (TCO) from other forms of criminality. This conceptual foundation is not academic formality; it is operational necessity. You cannot effectively combat what you do not understand.

I. Defining Transnational Organized Crime

1.1 Etymology and Core Concept

The phrase "transnational organized crime" contains three words, each carrying precise legal and analytical weight. Understanding them separately before combining them reveals why this category of threat requires a different response from conventional law enforcement.

The word crime derives from the Latin crimen, meaning accusation or wrongdoing — specifically, acts that harm not merely an individual victim but the community. In legal tradition, crimes are distinguished from civil wrongs precisely because their impact extends beyond private parties to the social order itself. This matters for our analysis: criminal organizations do not merely steal from individuals. They destabilize communities, corrupt institutions, and erode the foundations of civic life.

Organized, from the Greek organon (tool or instrument), implies deliberate structure, coordination, and purpose. An organized criminal group is not a spontaneous collection of individuals committing opportunistic acts. It is a structured enterprise with roles, hierarchy, protocols, and long-term strategic objectives. The organizational dimension is what transforms a group of criminals into a system — and systems are far more resilient, far more dangerous, and far harder to dismantle than collections of individuals.

Transnational is perhaps the most operationally significant term. It means literally "across nations" — and in organized crime, it signals that the group's activities, members, resources, or impact span more than one country. Transnationality is not merely a geographic descriptor. It is a structural advantage: it allows criminal organizations to arbitrage legal differences between jurisdictions, evade law enforcement through international mobility, and access markets unavailable to purely local groups. The border that protects a nation from foreign invasion is, paradoxically, a tool of evasion for transnational criminals.

1.2 The United Nations Definition — The Palermo Framework

The authoritative international legal definition of transnational organized crime is found in the United Nations Convention Against Transnational Organized Crime, commonly known as the Palermo Convention, adopted by the UN General Assembly in November 2000 and entered into force in September 2003. The United States ratified it in November 2005. This Convention remains the cornerstone of the international legal architecture against organized crime and the primary reference framework for U.S. federal agencies engaged in this work.

The Palermo Convention defines an "organized criminal group" as a structured group of three or more persons existing for a period and acting in concert with the aim of committing one or more serious crimes or offences established in accordance with this Convention, in order to get, directly or indirectly, a financial or other material benefit.

This definition, while foundational, is notably outcome-focused: it defines organized crime by what it does (structured group, serious crime, material benefit) rather than what it looks like internally. This is deliberate — the drafters recognized criminal organizations take radically different forms across cultures and contexts, and that a definition tied to specific organizational structures would be quickly circumvented.

For an offense to qualify as "transnational," the Convention requires that it be committed in more than one state; committed in one state but with substantial preparatory actions, planning, direction, or control in another; committed in one state but involving an organized criminal group that operates in more than one state; or committed in one state with substantial effects in another state.

The Tren de Aragua satisfies every element of this definition, a fact with significant legal and operational implications that will be explored in Chapter Eight.

1.3 The U.S. Federal Framework: From Presidential Strategy to Terrorist Designation

Beyond the Palermo Convention, U.S. domestic law and executive policy have developed a parallel — and rapidly evolving — framework for defining and combating transnational organized crime. Understanding this framework is essential for any law enforcement professional or security practitioner operating in the current environment, because the legal tools available to federal prosecutors and investigators have expanded significantly since 2025.

The foundational policy instrument remained, until recently, the July 2011 Strategy to Combat Transnational Organized Crime, issued during the Obama administration, which defined TCOs as "self-perpetuating associations of individuals who operate transnationally to obtain power, influence, monetary and/or commercial gains, wholly or in part by illegal means, while protecting their activities through a pattern of corruption and/or violence, or while protecting their illegal activities through a transnational organizational structure and the exploitation of transnational commerce or communication mechanisms." This definition established the analytical vocabulary that has governed interagency coordination on TCO threats for over a decade.

That framework was dramatically expanded on January 20, 2025, when President Donald Trump signed Executive Order 14157 — "Designating Cartels and Other Organizations as Foreign Terrorist Organizations and Specially Designated Global Terrorists" — on his first day in office. The Executive Order directed the Secretary of State, in consultation with the Attorney General and the Secretary of the Treasury, to evaluate whether to designate specific criminal organizations as Foreign Terrorist Organizations (FTOs) under Section 219 of the Immigration and Nationality Act (8 U.S.C. § 1189).

On February 20, 2025, acting on that directive, Secretary of State Marco Rubio formally designated the Tren de Aragua as a Foreign Terrorist Organization — a designation published in the Federal Register (FR Doc. 2025-02873) and carrying immediate legal consequences. The designation placed the Tren de Aragua in the same legal category as al-Qaeda and the Islamic State, triggering criminal liability for any person who knowingly provides material support to the organization, enabling financial sanctions against its members and associates, and facilitating enhanced coordination between domestic law enforcement and international intelligence partners.

On March 14, 2025, President Trump took the additional step of invoking the Alien Enemies Act of 1798 — only the fourth time in American history the Act has been invoked, and the first peacetime invocation — declaring that the Tren de Aragua constituted an "invasion" of the United States. On the next day, 238 Venezuelan nationals were deported by the administration to El Salvador's CECOT maximum-security prison. The legal validity of that invocation became the subject of extensive litigation: U.S. District Judge James Boasberg issued a temporary restraining order, and on September 2, 2025, a federal appellate court ruled that the Alien Enemies Act could not be used against the Tren de Aragua because the organization's activities did not constitute an "invasion or predatory incursion" within the Act's legal definition. On July 18, 2025, the men deported to CECOT were returned to Venezuela due to a prisoner exchange in which Venezuela liberated ten U.S. citizens and lawful permanent residents detained as political prisoners.

These legal developments are more than procedural history. They reveal a fundamental tension at the heart of U.S. policy on the Tren de Aragua — a tension that has direct operational implications for law enforcement and security professionals. The Trump administration's terrorist designation reflects a political judgment that the organization's threat level requires the most severe available legal response. Federal courts and the U.S. Intelligence Community have simultaneously cautioned that treating a profit-driven criminal organization as a state-sponsored terrorist group may rest on factual premises — including the claim of Venezuelan government direction of TdA operations — that the evidence does not fully support. A February 26, 2025, U.S. Intelligence Community assessment concluded with moderate confidence that the Venezuelan government was not directing Tren de Aragua operations in the United States. The FBI dissented, maintaining that the connection exists based on separate intelligence.

For the practitioner, this distinction matters operationally: a profit-motivated criminal franchise responds to different investigative and interdiction strategies than a state-sponsored terrorist organization. This book takes the position — based on over fifteen years of experience with Venezuelan criminal organizations — that the Tren de Aragua is best understood as a sophisticated transnational criminal enterprise with opportunistic relationships with state actors, not as a state-directed terrorist group. The terrorist designation, whatever its political utility, should not distort the analytical framework applied to actual field operations.

On the prosecutorial side, the RICO Act — the Racketeer Influenced and Corrupt Organizations Act, 18 U.S.C. §§ 1961-1968 — remains the primary federal tool for prosecuting transnational criminal organizations on U.S. soil. Since January 20, 2025, the Department of Justice has federally indicted over 260 members of the Tren de Aragua across five federal districts: Colorado, Nebraska, New Mexico, the Southern District of New York, and the Southern District of Texas. The Joint Task Force Vulcan (JTFV) — originally created in 2019 to combat MS-13 — was expanded by Attorney General Pamela Bondi to specifically target the Tren de Aragua, coordinating the FBI, DEA, HSI, ATF, U.S. Marshals Service, and the

Bureau of Prisons across a nationwide prosecution strategy. As of December 2025, JTFV operations span thirteen U.S. Attorney's Offices across the country.

The rapidly evolving legal framework surrounding the Tren de Aragua — from the 2011 TCO strategy to the 2025 terrorist designation, from RICO prosecutions to Alien Enemies Act invocations — underscores a central theme of this book: the organization has outpaced the institutional frameworks designed to contain it, forcing improvisation at the highest levels of American government. The chapters that follow provide the analytical foundation for a more coherent, evidence-based response.

II. Historical Evolution: From Local Gangs to Global Enterprises

2.1 Ancient Roots, Modern Transformation

Organized crime is not a modern invention. History records criminal associations operating with hierarchy, territory, and strategic purpose as far back as ancient Rome, where networks of bandits controlled trade routes and extracted tribute with remarkable organizational sophistication. Medieval piracy represented another form of proto-organized crime: maritime criminal enterprises with command structures, territorial claims, financial networks, and diplomatic relationships with sympathetic state actors.

What distinguishes modern transnational organized crime from these historical predecessors is not the fundamental human impulse toward organized predation — that is a constant — but the structural environment in which that impulse operates. Three macro-historical transformations have created the conditions for the unprecedented expansion of criminal enterprises in the 20th and 21st centuries: globalization, state fragility, and digital technology.

2.2 The Four Waves of Organized Crime

Security analysts have identified a useful framework for understanding the historical evolution of organized crime through four successive "waves," each building on the previous while adding additional dimensions of scale, sophistication, and reach. Understanding this progression is essential for placing the Tren de Aragua in its proper historical context — and for understanding why conventional law enforcement responses, designed for earlier waves, are inadequate against the current threat.

■ The First Wave: The Rise of the Mafia (Late 19th–Early 20th Century)

The first recognizable transnational criminal organizations emerged from the Italian Mafia tradition — the Sicilian Cosa Nostra, the Neapolitan Camorra, and the Calabrian 'Ndrangheta — which followed immigrant populations to the United States in the late 19th and early 20th centuries. These organizations pioneered the hierarchical structure that would become the template for criminal enterprises worldwide: a top-down chain of command, territorial monopolies, codes of silence (omertà), and the use of family and ethnic bonds as organizational glue. The first-wave model was characterized by rigidity — deep roots in specific communities, strong cultural identity, and limited geographic expansion. Its primary criminal markets were extortion, labor racketeering, and illicit gambling.

■ The Second Wave: The Narcotics Revolution (1970s–1990s)

The explosion of global drug trafficking, beginning in the 1970s, transformed organized crime from a local protection racket into a multibillion-dollar international industry. Colombian cartels — Medellín, Cali, and their successors — demonstrated that criminal organizations could generate revenues exceeding those of sovereign states, corrupt governments at the highest levels, deploy private military forces, and establish transnational logistics networks of staggering sophistication. The second wave introduced the "cartel model" characterized by commodity-specific focus (cocaine, heroin, marijuana), bilateral corruption — bribing officials at origin, transit, and destination countries — and extreme violence as a tool of market competition and state intimidation. The Colombian experience had profound consequences for the Western Hemisphere, establishing criminal infrastructure, corruption networks, and drug-market institutions that persist to this day.

■ The Third Wave: Globalization and Criminal Diversification (1990s–2010s)

The collapse of the Soviet Union, the liberalization of global trade, and the explosion of international migration created conditions for a third wave of organized crime characterized by unprecedented geographic mobility, criminal diversification, and organizational flexibility. Whereas second-wave organizations were commodity specialists, third-wave groups became criminal generalists — trafficking drugs, humans, weapons, and counterfeit goods through the same logistics networks. The dismantling of border controls within the European Union and the integration of global financial systems created both opportunities and vulnerabilities that criminal networks rapidly exploited. A defining feature of this era was the "networked" criminal organization, characterized by loosely affiliated cells linked through common interests, infrastructure, and communication, rather than a strict hierarchy.

■ The Fourth Wave: Digital Crime, Social Media, and the Franchise Model (2010s–Present)

The current wave of organized crime is defined by two converging forces: the digitization of criminal operations and the emergence of franchise-based organizational models. Digital platforms enable criminal recruitment, coordination, extortion, money laundering, and propaganda on a global scale from any smartphone. Social media has become a tool of criminal statecraft — organizations like the Tren de Aragua use TikTok, Instagram, and WhatsApp not merely for communication but for psychological operations, territorial assertion, and brand management. Simultaneously, the franchise model — pioneered by the Tren de Aragua and adopted by other criminal organizations — has replaced rigid hierarchy with adaptive decentralization: local cells operate with substantial autonomy under a shared brand, method, and leadership framework, making them simultaneously resilient against law enforcement disruption and capable of rapid geographic expansion.

III. What Makes a Criminal Organization "Organized"

3.1 The Structural Dimensions of Criminal Organization

Not all crime is organized crime. A burglar is not an organized criminal. A gang of street robbers operating in a single neighborhood is not, in the legal or analytical sense, a transnational organized crime group. Understanding the threshold that separates opportunistic criminality from organized crime is essential for accurate threat classification and appropriate resource allocation.

The criminological literature, synthesized across multiple scholarly traditions, identifies five structural dimensions that define organized crime as a distinct category of threat:

■ **Hierarchy and Structure**

Criminal organizations have defined leadership, chains of command, and role differentiation. Members have specific functions — leadership, logistics, enforcement, finance, recruitment — that persist regardless of which individual occupies them. This structural persistence is what makes criminal organizations resilient: the arrest or death of a leader does not destroy the organization because the structure remains and can accommodate a successor. The Tren de Aragua's "franquicia" (franchise) model represents an evolution of this principle: it distributes structural functions across semi-autonomous cells, reducing the organization's vulnerability to any single law enforcement action.

■ **Continuity Over Time**

Criminal organizations are designed to persist. Unlike conspiracies formed for a single criminal act, organized crime groups maintain their structure and operations across years and decades, surviving the loss of key members, law enforcement pressure, and changes in criminal markets. The Tren de Aragua has demonstrated remarkable institutional continuity: founded in the early 2000s inside a single Venezuelan prison, it has survived the death and arrest of multiple leaders, expanded across fifteen countries, and maintained its organizational coherence through radical environmental changes.

Use of Violence and Corruption as Institutional Tools

What distinguishes organized crime from other forms of enterprise — legal or illegal — is the systematic deployment of violence and corruption as operational instruments, not merely as occasional tactics. Violence establishes territorial control, enforces internal discipline, eliminates rivals, and intimidates witnesses. Corruption neutralizes state authority: when law enforcement officers, prosecutors, and judges are on the criminal payroll, the state's enforcement capacity is hollowed out from within. The Tren de Aragua has systematically deployed both tools in every country where it has established operations.

Market Orientation

Criminal organizations are economic actors. They identify and exploit market opportunities — typically in goods and services prohibited by law — and apply business logic to maximize returns. This market orientation drives the diversification of criminal portfolios: organizations that began with a single criminal commodity expand into adjacent markets as capital, logistics, and organizational capacity grow. The Tren de Aragua's criminal portfolio has expanded from prison extortion to human trafficking, sexual exploitation, contract killing, drug retail, loan sharking ("gota a gota"), kidnapping, and money laundering — each market leveraging the same organizational infrastructure.

■ Corruption of Public Institutions

The corruption of law enforcement, judicial, correctional, and political institutions is not a byproduct of organized crime's success; it is a strategic objective. Criminal organizations understand that state authority is their primary constraint, and they devote substantial resources to neutralizing it. The consequence is what scholars call "state capture": the gradual subordination of public institutions to criminal interests, creating a parallel governance structure that operates through — and increasingly instead of — legitimate authority. Venezuela's experience with the Tren de Aragua, detailed in Chapter Two, represents one of the most dramatic examples of state capture in the contemporary Western Hemisphere.

IV. Theoretical Frameworks: How Scholars Explain Organized Crime

For law enforcement and security professionals, theoretical frameworks may seem like an academic luxury. They are essential tools: they shape how organizations are analyzed, how threats are assessed, and how countermeasures are designed. The following frameworks have directly influenced U.S. federal policy on transnational organized crime and inform the analytical method of this book.

4.1 The Positivist Framework: Crime as a Measurable Phenomenon

The positivist tradition, rooted in the 19th-century criminology of Cesare Lombroso and refined through a century of empirical social science, treats crime as a phenomenon with observable, measurable causes. From this perspective, organized crime can be analyzed through quantifiable indicators: arrest rates, seizure volumes, the geographic distribution of criminal activity, financial flows, and network topology. The positivist approach underpins the data collection and intelligence analysis frameworks used by agencies including the DEA, FBI, and DHS in tracking transnational criminal organizations.

The strength of positivist analysis is its empirical rigor and its compatibility with intelligence-sharing and database systems. Its limitation is that raw data rarely captures the organizational logic, cultural dynamics, and adaptive strategies that determine how criminal organizations actually function. The Tren de Aragua is a case in point: its criminal portfolio is not explainable by analyzing seizure data alone — understanding it requires analyzing the organizational culture, prison socialization processes, and migration dynamics that shaped the group's development.

4.2 The Sociological Framework: Crime as a Social Phenomenon

Sociological criminology — associated with scholars including Émile Durkheim and Robert Merton — understands organized crime not as the product of individual pathology but as a predictable response to structural conditions: economic inequality, weak institutions, limited legitimate opportunity, and social anomie. From this perspective, the Tren de Aragua is not an aberration but a product of Venezuela's specific historical conditions: a prison system without rule of law, an economy in collapse, a state hollowed out by corruption, and a massive migration crisis that created populations of exceptional vulnerability.

This framework has direct operational value. If organized crime is produced by structural conditions, then those conditions can — in principle — be modified. The policy recommendations in Chapter Ten draw on sociological analysis to identify interventions that address criminal organizations at their roots rather than merely their branches.

4.3 The Systems Framework: Crime as an Adaptive Network

The systems theory perspective — applied to criminology through the work of Niklas Luhmann and expanded by security scholars — understands criminal organizations as complex adaptive systems: networks of interrelated elements that respond dynamically to changes in their environment. From this perspective, the Tren de Aragua's extraordinary geographic expansion is not the result of deliberate strategic planning by a central command but an emergent property of the organization's adaptive structure: each cell responds to local conditions, exploits local vulnerabilities, and connects to the broader network through shared identity, method, and communication.

The systems framework has profound implications for countermeasure design. If a criminal organization is a complex adaptive system, then targeting individual leaders — the traditional law enforcement approach — is insufficient: the system adapts and reconstitutes around the disruption. Effective countermeasures must target the system's structural properties: the communication networks, financial flows, and institutional corruption that hold the organization together. This analysis informs the strategic recommendations in Chapter Ten.

V. The Transnational Dimension: Why Borders Are a Criminal Advantage

The transnational dimension of criminal organizations is not merely a geographic feature. It is a strategic asset that fundamentally alters the risk-reward calculus of criminal enterprise and creates systematic advantages over law enforcement agencies constrained by national jurisdiction.

5.1 Jurisdictional Arbitrage

Criminal organizations operating across multiple jurisdictions can structure their activities to minimize legal exposure: conducting the most legally sensitive operations in countries with weak enforcement capacity, routing financial flows through jurisdictions with inadequate anti-money-laundering frameworks, and maintaining leadership in countries with limited extradition cooperation. The inability of legal systems in one country to access evidence, records, and witnesses in another creates systematic investigative dead ends that criminal organizations deliberately exploit.

The Tren de Aragua's most consequential jurisdictional arbitrage involves Venezuela itself. The absence of functioning criminal records databases accessible to foreign law enforcement — a direct consequence of the Venezuelan state's institutional collapse — means that law enforcement agencies in the United States, Chile, Colombia, and Peru cannot verify whether individuals of Venezuelan origin have criminal histories in their country of origin. This information gap, analyzed in Chapters Seven and Eight, is one of the most significant operational challenges in combating the organization on American soil.

5.2 Migration as Operational Infrastructure

The mass migration of Venezuelan nationals — estimated at over seven million people by 2024, representing the largest displacement crisis in the Western Hemisphere — created infrastructure that the Tren de Aragua has systematically exploited. Migration routes, border crossings, refugee camps, migrant shelters, and diaspora communities are not merely the settings in which criminal activity occurs; they are the operational logistics network through which the organization moves personnel, resources, and victims across international borders.

This exploitation of migration infrastructure is one of the Tren de Aragua's most distinctive organizational features and one of the most important for U.S. law enforcement to understand. The criminals do not operate in spite of the humanitarian crisis — they operate through it, using the same channels, disguised among the same populations, exploiting the same institutional gaps. Disentangling the criminal network from the humanitarian crisis it inhabits — without criminalizing the millions of legitimate Venezuelan migrants who are themselves the organization's primary victims — is one of the central operational and policy challenges of this book.

VI. The Socioeconomic and Political Impact of Transnational Organized Crime

The damage inflicted by transnational organized crime extends far beyond the immediate victims of individual criminal acts. The systemic effects on governance, economic development, public health, and democratic institutions have been the subject of extensive research by international bodies, including the UN, the Inter-American Development Bank, and the World Bank. Understanding this broader impact is essential for making the case — to legislators, policymakers, and the public — for the institutional resources required to combat organizations like the Tren de Aragua effectively.

6.1 Governance and Institutional Corruption

The corruption of public institutions by criminal organizations imposes costs that extend far beyond any individual corrupt transaction. When police officers are on criminal payrolls, crimes go unreported and uninvestigated. When prosecutors are intimidated or bought, criminal cases collapse or are never filed. When judges render decisions in favor of criminal defendants, the entire judicial system loses legitimacy. The cumulative effect is what political scientists call "state capture" — the subordination of public institutions to private criminal interests, effectively replacing the rule of law with the rule of the criminal network.

Venezuela's experience with this process — and its implications for the Tren de Aragua's development — will be examined in depth in Chapter Two. For now, it is sufficient to note that state capture in the country of origin is directly relevant to U.S. law enforcement: it is precisely because the Venezuelan state cannot or will not cooperate in providing criminal intelligence and records that American agencies face such severe information asymmetries when dealing with Venezuelan criminal organizations operating on U.S. soil.

6.2 Economic Distortion

Criminal organizations distort legitimate economic activity in multiple, overlapping ways. Extortion — the Tren de Aragua's foundational revenue mechanism — functions as an informal tax on legitimate businesses, reducing profit margins, discouraging investment, and driving enterprises out of affected areas. Money laundering — the conversion of criminal proceeds into ostensibly legitimate assets — distorts real estate markets, retail businesses, and financial institutions. The Inter-American Development

Bank estimated in 2024 that Latin America and the Caribbean recorded approximately 20 homicides per 100,000 inhabitants, a rate more than triple the global average, with organized crime the primary driver.

6.3 Human Cost: The Victims

Statistics, however necessary, can obscure the human reality of organized crime's impact. The Tren de Aragua's primary victims — migrants, women subjected to sexual exploitation, business owners forced to pay extortion, community members living under criminal territorial control — are not abstractions. They are the reason this book exists. Throughout the following chapters, the analytical narrative will be anchored in specific documented cases that give concrete human form to the statistical trends.

This human-centered approach is not merely ethical; it is operationally important. Law enforcement agencies that understand the specific human experiences of criminal victimization are better equipped to develop victim-centered investigative approaches, build community trust in affected diaspora populations, and design prevention programs that address the actual vulnerabilities that criminal organizations exploit.

VII. Key Terms and Definitions for This Book

The following definitions are used consistently throughout this text. They draw on the Palermo Convention, U.S. federal statutes, and established criminological scholarship. Readers familiar with some of these terms from other contexts should note the specific usage adopted here, which may differ from colloquial or journalistic usage.

- **Transnational Criminal Organization (TCO)**

  A structured group of three or more persons that has existed for a significant period, acts in concert, engages in serious criminal activity, seeks financial or material benefit, and operates in more than one country or has transnational effects. The Tren de Aragua is a TCO in this precise legal and analytical sense.

- **Franquicia Criminal (Criminal Franchise)**

  The organizational model pioneered by the Tren de Aragua, in which semi-autonomous local cells operate under a shared brand, identity, operational method, and loose leadership oversight, without requiring direct command-and-control from a central authority. This model distinguishes the Tren de Aragua from traditional hierarchical criminal organizations and has significant implications for its resilience against law enforcement disruption.

- **Pran**

The term used within Venezuelan prison culture to denote the de facto leader of a prison cell block or facility — the head of the criminal governance structure that substituted for legitimate correctional authority. The pran system was the organizational incubator from which the Tren de Aragua developed. Understanding this system is essential to understanding the organization's internal culture, communication codes, and authority structures.

- **Vacuna (Vaccine)**

  The colloquial term used by the Tren de Aragua and related Venezuelan criminal organizations for the extortion payments demanded from businesses, residents, and other individuals operating in territories under the organization's control. The term reflects the criminal organization's implicit offer: payment provides "protection" from the violence the organization itself threatens. This protection racket is one of the organization's primary revenue mechanisms in both Venezuela and the diaspora communities where it has established operations.

- **Diáspora (Diaspora)**

  The Venezuelan diaspora refers to the over seven million Venezuelan nationals who have emigrated from Venezuela since 2015, driven by political repression, economic collapse, and a humanitarian crisis. This population — distributed across Latin America, North America, Europe, and beyond — is simultaneously the Tren de Aragua's primary victim pool and its primary cover. The organization exploits diaspora communities by positioning its members within them and by targeting diaspora members whose undocumented status makes them reluctant to contact law enforcement.

■ **Gobernanza Criminal (Criminal Governance)**
The phenomenon by which criminal organizations substitute for legitimate state authority in controlling territory, resolving disputes, providing (coercive) security, and extracting resources from populations. The Tren de Aragua first developed criminal governance within Venezuela's prison system — effectively administering prisons that the state had ceded to criminal control — and subsequently extended this model to neighborhoods, border zones, and diaspora communities in multiple countries.

VIII. Chapter Summary and Forward Look

This chapter has established the conceptual foundation necessary for the analysis that follows. We have defined transnational organized crime through the authoritative frameworks of the Palermo Convention and U.S. federal policy, traced the historical evolution of criminal organizations through four successive waves, identified the structural dimensions that distinguish organized crime from other forms of criminality, and examined the theoretical frameworks that inform this book's analytical approach.

Two themes have emerged that will recur throughout the following chapters:

First, the Tren de Aragua is not an anomaly. It is the product of specific historical, institutional, and structural conditions that can be analyzed, understood, and — with appropriate intervention — disrupted. The analytical frameworks introduced in this chapter provide the tools for this analysis.

Second, the organization's transnational dimension is not merely a geographic feature but a strategic asset that creates systematic advantages over law enforcement agencies constrained by national jurisdiction. Countering it requires an equally transnational and cross-jurisdictional response — one that this book's final chapters will outline in concrete operational and policy terms.

Chapter Two turns to the source: Venezuela itself. Before the Tren de Aragua could become an international criminal organization, it had to be born — in a prison, within a state, inside a political and institutional crisis that created the conditions for its extraordinary development. Understanding that origin is not historical background. It is operational intelligence.

— END OF CHAPTER ONE —

CHAPTER TWO

Venezuela: The State That Incubated the Monster

Institutional collapse, criminal capture of state power, and the fall of the Maduro regime

Author's Note: What Only a Venezuelan Prosecutor Can Say

I write this chapter from a vantage point no outside analyst can occupy. I served as a prosecutor in Venezuela's Public Ministry for over fifteen years. I witnessed firsthand how the institutions I swore to protect were hollowed out, corrupted, and ultimately captured. I knew the Venezuelan penitentiary system from the inside — not as an academic observer, but as an officer of the court who prosecuted criminals who then returned to the same facilities that had shaped them.

When outside observers speak of Venezuela's "institutional collapse," they speak in the language of statistics, corruption indices, and international organization reports. When you live it from within, what you see is different: a judge who suddenly stops convicting defendants with government ties. A case file that disappears from the archive. A witness who withdraws testimony without explanation. A colleague who warns you in hushed tones that certain cases are better left unpursued. That gradual process — that slow death of the rule of law — is what this chapter describes. It is essential context for understanding how a prison gang became a transnational criminal empire.

And I write with renewed urgency because on January 3, 2026, Nicolas Maduro was captured by U.S. special forces in Caracas and transported to New York to face federal charges that include, among others, his direct complicity with the Tren de Aragua. What for years had been documented evidence assembled by prosecutors, human rights activists, and investigative journalists now carries the weight of a formal indictment from the Southern District of New York. This chapter tells the story of how we arrived at that historic moment.

I. Venezuela Before the Collapse: The State That Was

To understand the magnitude of Venezuela's institutional collapse — and why that collapse was the precondition for the emergence of the Tren de Aragua — it is essential to recall what Venezuela was before it fell. This is not nostalgia; it is precision. Measuring the distance between the starting point and the destination measures the depth of institutional destruction.

For most of the twentieth century, Venezuela had one of the most developed judicial systems in Latin America. The Constitution of 1961 — the product of a democratic pact between the country's principal political forces known as the Punto Fijo Pact — established a framework of separation of powers, individual rights, and rule of law that, while imperfect in its application, was real in its structure. The Public Ministry operated with relative independence. Courts processed cases with a degree of predictability. The penitentiary system, though chronically deficient, was administered by the state.

The world's largest proven oil reserves made Venezuela one of Latin America's most prosperous nations for decades. By 1970, Venezuela had the highest per capita income in the region. Caracas was known as the "city of skyscrapers," and the Venezuelan middle class traveled to Miami to shop with a frequency that became proverbial. That relative prosperity, sustained by oil revenue, contained its own vulnerability: when the state depends on oil, its institutions depend on the same resource. When oil becomes a political instrument, institutions become its first victims.

1.1 The Chavez Legacy: Revolution and Institutional Co-optation

Hugo Chavez to power in 1999 marked the beginning of the process that, two decades later, would produce the perfect conditions for the emergence of the Tren de Aragua. The Chavista process was not an instantaneous institutional collapse: it was a systematic, gradual, and deliberate Co-optation of every state institution — from the judiciary to the armed forces, from the penitentiary system to the Public Ministry itself.

The Constitution of 1999, approved by referendum with broad popular support, replaced the previous institutional framework with one that concentrated executive power to an unprecedented degree in Venezuelan democratic history. The Supreme Court progressively filled with government-aligned justices. Independent prosecutors were replaced by political loyalists. The armed forces were politicized through Bolivarian doctrine and the incorporation of military officers into civilian and commercial positions.

But perhaps the decision with the most lasting consequences for public security was adopted regarding the penitentiary system. Faced with chronic overcrowding and endemic violence in Venezuelan prisons, the Chavista government chose not to reform the system but to reach a tacit agreement: to cede internal control of prisons to the highest-ranking inmates — the pranes — in exchange for those leaders maintaining a minimum of order and avoiding mass confrontations with the state. That decision planted the seed of catastrophe.

> *Author's Note: As a prosecutor, I witnessed how this tacit agreement operated in practice. Inmates with the greatest organizational power received privileges, communication access, and relative freedom of movement. Prison authorities looked the other way. The consequence was predictable: prisons became command centers for criminal operations extending far beyond their walls. Cases that should have led to systemic reform instead led to plea negotiations with the very leaders of the criminal structures inside.*

II. The Pranato System: How the State Lost Control of Its Own Prisons

2.1 The Origin of the Venezuelan Pranato

The term "pran" — an acronym popularized as "Preso Rematado Asesino Nato" (roughly, "born-killer convicted prisoner") — describes the de facto leader of a Venezuelan prison cell block or facility. The pran system did not originate with Chavismo: its roots reach back to the 1990s, when chronic overcrowding and resource scarcity made effective state control of prisons practically impossible. But it was under Chavismo that the system evolved from a tolerated reality into a functional instrument of state policy.

The critical events that institutionalized the pranato occurred in 2011. In May of that year, a 26-year-old prison leader known as "Oriente" — Yorvis Valentin Lopez Cortez — held off over 4,000 Venezuelan security forces, including tanks and helicopters, for 27 days during a siege of El Rodeo prison, on the outskirts of Caracas. The government ultimately secured the facility — but not before Oriente escaped in what multiple sources described as a backroom arrangement with then-Interior Minister Tareck El Aissami. The official narrative of a law enforcement victory obscured what was, in operational terms, a negotiated capitulation.

The 2011 El Rodeo riots paradoxically produced the opposite of what they should have generated. Rather than serious penitentiary reform, the government created a Ministry of Penitentiary Services — under Iris Varela — that used the incident as a pretext for a "prison peace" model that legitimized the pranes as institutional interlocutors of the state. The criminological consequence was predictable and devastating: the formalization of a parallel authority structure inside Venezuelan prisons that would become the organizational incubator of the Tren de Aragua.

2.2 Tareck El Aissami: The Architect of the Permissive Environment

No figure is more central to understanding the incubation of the Tren de Aragua within the Venezuelan state apparatus than Tareck El Aissami. A lawyer and criminologist by training — with studies at the University of the Andes — El Aissami served as Minister of Interior and Justice from 2008 to 2012, precisely the period during which he oversaw the penitentiary system that created the pranato's conditions. He was subsequently appointed Governor of Aragua state — the state where Tocorón prison is located — from 2012 to 2017.

The criminological and operational significance of this geographic and institutional overlap cannot be overstated. The man who, as Interior Minister, had tolerated and formalized the pran system became the governor of the state that housed the Tren de Aragua's incubator. Under his gubernatorial tenure, violence in Aragua state surged, transforming it into one of Venezuela's most dangerous jurisdictions, while Tocorón prison was quietly converted into the command headquarters of a criminal organization in formation.

On February 13, 2017 — just weeks after being appointed Executive Vice President of the Republic by Maduro — the U.S. Department of the Treasury designated El Aissami as a Specially Designated Narcotics Trafficker under the Foreign Narcotics Kingpin Act, freezing his U.S. assets and revoking his visa. Maduro kept El Aissami in government for over a year after that designation. El Aissami was eventually arrested in Venezuela in April 2024 on corruption charges related to the PDVSA-Crypto scheme. He remains detained in Venezuela as this book goes to press.

2.3 Tocorón: The Prison That Became a Criminal City

To understand the Tren de Aragua, one must understand Tocorón. The Aragua Penitentiary Center — colloquially known as "Tocorón" or "Casa Grande" — was for over a decade not simply a troubled prison but a state within a state: a sovereign territory with its own governance system, its own economy, its own security force, and its own transnational criminal foreign policy.

Under the leadership of Hector Rusthenford Guerrero Flores — "Niño Guerrero" — who returned to Tocorón shortly after Maduro's 2013 presidential election victory to serve time for the murder of a police officer, the prison was literally rebuilt. When the Venezuelan military finally raided Tocorón in September 2023, the images that emerged from the facility stunned the world: swimming pools, a professional baseball field, a zoo with tigers and caimans, a nightclub, restaurants, gaming rooms, and war-grade weaponry. All inside the walls of a Venezuelan state prison.

Inmates paid weekly dues — called "la causa" — that generated approximately $3.5 million annually from the incarcerated population alone. But the real revenue flowed from criminal operations planned and coordinated from within: extortion, human trafficking, contract killing, money laundering. Guards were bribed. Families visited freely. Telephone and internet communications operated without restriction. By every practical measure, Tocorón was the corporate headquarters of a transnational criminal enterprise that the Venezuelan state not only permitted but, according to growing evidence, actively facilitated.

■ **The Tocorón Organizational Architecture**
"Trenes" (trains) were the primary organizational units — groups of inmates under shared leadership. Each train subdivided into "carros" (cars): specialized operational cells with distinct functions — finance, security, communications, external operations. The pran — Niño Guerrero — headed the supreme hierarchy, with

lieutenants administering distinct areas of criminal activity. This organizational model — modular, hierarchical at the apex but decentralized in execution — became the template the organization replicated in every country where it subsequently established operations. The vocabulary itself — tren, carro, pran — traveled with the organization as it went global, allowing law enforcement agencies who understand this lexicon to identify organizational affiliation even in the absence of documentary evidence.

III. From Prison Walls to the Streets: The First Expansion

3.1 Criminal Governance Extends to Neighborhoods

The Tren de Aragua's first expansion was not transnational; it was territorial. Before crossing international borders, the organization extended its criminal governance model to the communities surrounding Tocorón and, progressively, to barrios across Caracas and other Venezuelan states. This intermediate stage is criminologically significant: it allowed the organization to refine its operational method, test its franchise model, and develop the human capital that would later be deployed internationally.

The mechanism was straightforward and brutal. Members who completed sentences or were "strategically transferred" to other facilities carried with them the Tren de Aragua's structure, codes, and loyalties. In the neighborhoods where they settled, they replicated the prison model: establishing territories, imposing the "vacuna" (extortion tax) on businesses and residents, recruiting unemployed youth, and using extreme violence as an instrument of control and terror. Front organizations — such as the "Fundacion Somos El Barrio JK" — operated as charitable facades that legitimized the gang's community presence before authorities and neighbors alike.

From a law enforcement perspective, this territorial expansion phase offers a critical lesson: the Tren de Aragua developed its governance capacity not through sudden institutional capture but through a process of gradual territorial consolidation that Venezuelan authorities allowed to proceed unchallenged. The same permissive environment that had created the pranato inside prisons created it outside them. When law enforcement agencies in the United States encounter the Tren de Aragua operating in diaspora communities, they are observing an organization that has refined this method across many years and many jurisdictions.

3.2 Economic Collapse as a Criminal Accelerant

The permissive institutional environment that enabled the Tren de Aragua's growth was exponentially amplified by Venezuela's economic implosion beginning in 2014. The dramatic collapse of oil prices, compounded by the catastrophic economic mismanagement of the Maduro government, produced the most severe hyperinflationary episode in the Western Hemisphere in the twenty-first century.

By 2016, Venezuela was experiencing annual inflation exceeding 700 percent. By 2018, that figure had surpassed 1,700,000 percent. Salaries evaporated within days of being paid. Hospitals lacked basic medications. Supermarket shelves were bare. Child malnutrition reached levels unseen in Venezuela in living memory. The Inter-American Development Bank reported that by 2022, Latin America and the Caribbean recorded approximately 20 homicides per 100,000 inhabitants — a rate more than triple the global average — with Venezuela among the region's most extreme cases.

For the Tren de Aragua, this economic collapse represented an exceptional operational opportunity across three dimensions. First, it dramatically expanded the pool of potential recruits: young Venezuelans with no prospects in the formal economy who were susceptible to the income, protection, and belonging that criminal organizations offer. Second, it created ideal victims: families desperate enough to accept usurious "gota a gota" loans, businesses vulnerable enough to pay extortion as an alternative to closure, and individuals isolated enough from institutional protection to be exploited without recourse. Third, it generated the mass migration that would become the organization's primary transnational logistics infrastructure.

IV. Transnationalization: Following the Diaspora

4.1 The Largest Displacement Crisis in the Western Hemisphere

The Venezuelan emigration wave beginning in 2015 represented one of the largest population movements in the Western Hemisphere's history. By 2025, over 7.8 million Venezuelans — approximately 25 percent of the country's population — had abandoned the national territory. That population distributed primarily across Colombia (over 2.8 million), Peru (over 1.5 million), Ecuador, Chile, Brazil, Argentina, Panama, Mexico, and the United States.

What from a humanitarian perspective was a tragedy of unprecedented scale in Venezuelan history was, from a criminal perspective, an exceptional logistical opportunity. The Tren de Aragua had developed its organizational architecture within Venezuela's penitentiary system. Now that structure had access to a transnational human mobility network of millions of people, with established routes, known crossing points, and — most critically — a population of extreme vulnerability.

Venezuelan migration routes — the Troncal 5 highway toward the Colombian border, the Darién Gap toward Panama, the irregular border crossings at dozens of frontier points — became the Tren de Aragua's criminal corridors. First as migration facilitators — "coyotes" who charged to guide migrants through dangerous passages — and then as extortionists, traffickers, and exploiters of those same people. The organization monetized both the facilitation and the victimization of the same human flow, extracting revenue at every stage of the migration journey.

4.2 Expansion as Venezuelan State Policy: The Evidence

One of the most contested — and, in the light of evidence, most substantiated — assertions about the Tren de Aragua is that its transnational expansion was not merely an autonomous development tolerated by the

Venezuelan state, but in part a deliberate instrument of the Maduro regime's foreign policy. This is a serious claim that demands serious evidence, and the evidence, while not conclusive in every dimension, is substantial.

The most thoroughly documented case is the assassination of Venezuelan Lieutenant Ronald Ojeda in Santiago, Chile, on February 21, 2024. Ojeda — a 32-year-old dissident military officer who had fled Venezuela and publicly expressed opposition to the regime — was abducted from his Santiago apartment by individuals posing as Chilean police officers. His body was recovered nine days later. Chilean prosecutors' investigations determined that the murder was executed by members of the Tren de Aragua with documented links to the Maduro regime. One suspect had served as a personal security operative for Tareck El Aissami during his tenure as Governor of Aragua state.

The Human Rights Foundation's April 2025 report concluded categorically that "the Maduro regime has weaponized a prison-born megabanda into an agile paramilitary tool that serves as an instrument of transnational repression." The analysis advanced by security researchers at the Secure Free Society Initiative describes a strategy in which the Tren de Aragua served as Venezuela's "deniable vector of disorder" — deployed against Lima Group countries that supported sanctions against Maduro, generating instability that overwhelmed local security forces, redirected political debate from sanctions policy to street-level insecurity, and imposed costs on governments pledged to isolate the Venezuelan regime.

> *Author's Note: As a legal professional with direct experience in the Venezuelan system, I must make an important analytical distinction. There is a difference between the evidence that the Venezuelan state created the conditions for the Tren de Aragua's growth — which is clear and abundant — and the assertion that the Maduro regime operationally directed the organization's transnational expansion, which is a plausible hypothesis supported by significant circumstantial evidence but one that the U.S. Intelligence Community has evaluated with caution. The January 2026 federal indictment presents the prosecutorial theory; it is the judicial process that will determine the facts. This book presents the evidence with analytical rigor, not as political advocacy for any position.*

V. The Historic Reckoning: The Capture of Maduro, January 3, 2026

5.1 Operation Absolute Resolve: What Happened

In the early morning hours of Saturday, January 3, 2026, U.S. special operations forces executed Operation Absolute Resolve in Caracas, Venezuela. In an operation coordinated with the support of the Department of Justice and the Central Intelligence Agency, Nicolas Maduro Moros and his wife Cilia Flores were taken into custody and transported to the USS Iwo Jima, before being flown to Stewart Air National Guard Base in New York State.

The operation marked the fourth time in American history that the executive branch had conducted an extraterritorial apprehension of a foreign head of state — and the first time the target was a sitting president with an active electoral mandate, however contested. It represented the most dramatic extraterritorial law enforcement action in the Western Hemisphere since the capture of Panamanian strongman Manuel Noriega in 1989 — and, unlike the Noriega operation, it was conducted without a prior formal declaration of war or congressional authorization, relying instead on the President's Article II authority and the outstanding federal arrest warrants dating from the 2020 indictment.

On the same day as the capture, the Department of Justice — with Attorney General Pamela Bondi at the helm — unsealed a superseding indictment in the Southern District of New York that expanded and updated the charges originally filed in March 2020. President Trump confirmed the operation from his Mar-a-Lago club, declaring Maduro "one of the world's most notorious narco-traffickers." Attorney General Bondi described him as a "threat to national security" and declared that "the days of impunity for Venezuela's criminal leadership are over."

5.2 The Defendants: Who Is Named in the Indictment

The January 3, 2026 superseding indictment names six defendants whose identities, read together, constitute a comprehensive map of the Venezuelan criminal state as the DOJ understands it:

■ **Nicolas Maduro Moros**

Former President of Venezuela. Charged as the apex of a narco-terrorism conspiracy spanning over 25 years. The indictment alleges he "sits atop a corrupt, illegitimate government that, for decades, has leveraged government power to protect and promote illegal activity, including drug trafficking." Currently in federal custody at the Metropolitan Detention Center in Brooklyn, New York. Pleaded not guilty on January 5, 2026.

- **Cilia Flores**

  First Lady of Venezuela and former President of the National Assembly. Charged with cocaine importation conspiracy and weapons offenses. The indictment alleges she accepted hundreds of thousands of dollars in bribes in 2007 to arrange a meeting between a large-scale drug trafficker and the director of Venezuela's National Anti-Drug Office. Pleaded not guilty on January 5, 2026. Currently detained alongside her husband.

- **Diosdado Cabello Rondon**

  Current Minister of Interior, Justice and Peace; described in the indictment as "one of the most powerful officials in Venezuela." Co-founder of the country's "street muscle" militia networks and vice president of the ruling party. Charged as a central figure in the narco-terrorism and cocaine trafficking conspiracies. Remains at large in Venezuela.

- **Ramon Rodriguez Chacin**

  Former Minister of Interior and Justice. Charged with making multiple trips to coordinate directly with FARC leadership at Miraflores presidential palace and Fuerte Tiuna military complex between 2018 and 2019. A key logistical link, according to the indictment, between the Venezuelan government and Colombian narco-terrorist organizations.

- **Nicolas Maduro Guerra ("Nicolasito")**

  Son of Nicolas Maduro; member of Venezuela's National Assembly. Including the president's own son as a co-defendant underscores the DOJ's theory of a family criminal enterprise at the apex of the Venezuelan state. Remains at large.

- **Hector Rusthenford Guerrero Flores ("Nino Guerrero")**
Alleged leader of the Tren de Aragua. His inclusion in the same indictment as the former president of Venezuela and his senior government officials is the single most consequential element of the January 3 indictment from a law enforcement and policy perspective. It represents the prosecutorial position that the leader of a transnational criminal organization and the head of a sovereign state were co-conspirators in the same criminal enterprise. Remains at large. Whereabouts unknown as of publication.

5.3 The Four Charges: What the Indictment Alleges

The superseding indictment presents four categories of charges against Maduro and his co-defendants. Each charge carries significant mandatory minimum sentences under federal law:

- **Count 1: Narco-Terrorism Conspiracy (18 U.S.C. § 2332g)**
The indictment alleges a conspiracy spanning over 25 years to use drug trafficking as a weapon against the United States, coordinating with multiple foreign terrorist organizations — including the FARC, ELN, Sinaloa Cartel, and Tren de Aragua — to flood American communities with cocaine. The narco-terrorism statute is specifically designed for cases where drug trafficking is used as an

instrument of violence or terror against a sovereign nation, making it distinct from conventional drug trafficking charges. Conviction carries a mandatory life imprisonment.

■ Count 2: Cocaine Importation Conspiracy (21 U.S.C. § 963)

The indictment details specific operations across two decades, including the use of diplomatic passports to facilitate drug transshipment, exploitation of the "presidential hangar" for cocaine shipments, and documented seizures by Mexican and French authorities that are traced back to Venezuelan government-protected networks. The indictment alleges that "for over 25 years, leaders of Venezuela have abused their positions of public trust and corrupted once-legitimate institutions to import tons of cocaine into the United States." The State Department estimated 200-250 tons of cocaine transiting Venezuela annually.

■ Count 3: Possession of Machine Guns and Destructive Devices (18 U.S.C. § 924(c))

This charge reflects the military dimension of the alleged scheme, including the provision of war-grade weaponry to terrorist and criminal organizations, the maintenance of private paramilitary units, and the use of the Venezuelan state security apparatus as a protection instrument for drug trafficking networks.

■ Count 4: Conspiracy to Possess Machine Guns and Destructive Devices

The conspiracy element of the weapons charge extends criminal liability to those who agreed to the acquisition and deployment of military-grade weapons even if not in direct physical possession, broadening the prosecutorial reach to all co-defendants named in the indictment.

5.4 The First Court Appearance: January 5, 2026

On Monday, January 5, 2026, Nicolas Maduro and Cilia Flores appeared before U.S. District Judge Alvin Hellerstein at the Daniel Patrick Moynihan United States Courthouse in Manhattan — the same courthouse that has processed some of the most significant federal criminal cases in American history, including the Gotti RICO trial and the sentencing of El Chapo Guzman.

The hearing was brief but historic. Maduro, transported under heavy guard from the Metropolitan Detention Center in Brooklyn by motorcade and helicopter, declared in Spanish: "I was kidnapped. I am innocent and a decent man — the president of my country. I am a prisoner of war." His attorney, Barry J. Pollack, argued that his client was "the head of a sovereign state entitled to the privileges that status ensures" and signaled that "voluminous" pretrial filings would address the legality of the military operation. Both Maduro and Flores entered not guilty pleas to all charges.

The legal proceedings that will follow are expected to be among the most complex and consequential in the history of the Southern District of New York — and in the history of international criminal law. Questions of sovereign immunity, the extraterritorial reach of U.S. law, the legality of the military capture, and the admissibility of evidence obtained through CIA and DOJ intelligence operations will all be litigated before any trial on the merits can begin. As of publication, the proceedings remain in their early stages.

5.5 The Strength of the Case: An Independent Legal Assessment

Setting aside the political dimensions of the capture operation, the legal case itself has received assessments from independent legal experts that are notably more favorable than the typical politically charged indictment. Adam Pollock, a former Assistant Attorney General of New York and managing partner of Pollock Cohen, reviewed the full indictment and described it as "a real indictment" — explicitly contrasting it with what he characterized as more overtly political prosecutions: "You're dealing with the Southern District of New York, the United States Attorney's Office, which is a really serious office that doesn't bring trumped-up political charges."

The indictment's strength derives from several evidentiary pillars. First, it references specific documented events — seizures by Mexican and French authorities, the arrest and conviction of Cilia Flores' nephews in New York — that are a matter of independent public record, providing an evidentiary foundation that is not dependent solely on government witnesses or intelligence assessments. Second, the level of operational detail — specific meetings, payments, and logistical arrangements — suggests the existence of cooperating witnesses and potentially recorded communications. Third, the 25-year time span of the alleged conspiracy creates a pattern-of-racketeering foundation that is highly compatible with RICO prosecution theory, even if the narco-terrorism statute is the primary charge.

5.6 The Intelligence-Prosecution Tension: A Critical Analytical Note

The most analytically significant aspect of the January 3 indictment for security practitioners is its explicit inclusion of Nino Guerrero as a co-conspirator of Maduro. This element sits in direct tension with the official assessment of the U.S. Intelligence Community.

A February 26, 2025 Intelligence Community assessment concluded with moderate confidence that the Venezuelan government was not controlling the Tren de

Aragua, the gang was not acting on government orders, and the regime lacked the resources and organizational coherence to direct the band's operations. A more comprehensive National Intelligence Council assessment in March 2025 also found no evidence that the Venezuelan government coordinated or systematically directed TdA movements to the United States. The FBI dissented from both assessments, maintaining that evidence of a connection exists based on separate intelligence.

This tension between the prosecutorial theory of the indictment and the IC assessment is not a contradiction to be dismissed — it is a signal to be understood. Criminal prosecutions operate under a different evidentiary logic than intelligence assessments: they present the strongest available case for conviction, while intelligence assessments aggregate and weigh all available information, including information that may be inconsistent with the prosecutorial narrative. Both are legitimate exercises within their respective domains. For the operational practitioner, the IC assessment offers the more reliable baseline for analytical work, while the indictment identifies the prosecutorial theory that will shape federal interdiction strategy.

This book takes the evidence-anchored position, stated in Chapter One, that the Tren de Aragua is best understood as a sophisticated profit-motivated criminal franchise with opportunistic state relationships — not as a state-directed terrorist organization. The Maduro indictment does not alter that analytical conclusion, though it establishes that the boundary between criminal enterprise and state apparatus in Venezuela was far more porous than conventional governance analysis acknowledges.

VI. The New Landscape: Venezuela After the Capture

6.1 The Transitional Government: Delcy Rodriguez and Institutional Uncertainty

The capture of Maduro on January 3, 2026 left Venezuela in an unprecedented power vacuum. Vice President Delcy Rodriguez assumed the role of acting president under simultaneous pressure from the international community, the economic blockade maintained by the United States, and internal mobilization by Venezuelan civil society actors who saw in Maduro's capture a historic window for democratic transition.

Beginning January 8, 2026, the Rodriguez administration announced the release of political prisoners — a signal of negotiated transition rather than continuity of repression. By March 8, 2026, Foro Penal, Venezuela's primary human rights NGO monitoring political prisoners, had confirmed the release of 621 political detainees, with over 500 remaining according to human rights organization estimates. In President Trump's 2026 State of the Union address, he celebrated Maduro's capture and invited Venezuelan politician Enrique Marquez — released from detention in January — as a special guest to the ceremony.

However, the UN Human Rights Council's Independent International Fact-Finding Mission on Venezuela issued a stark warning in March 2026: the "repressive state" structures remained intact after Maduro's capture, and since January 3, 87 new politically motivated arrests had been documented. The machinery of Chavismo — constructed over a quarter century — does not automatically dismantle itself with the removal of its principal leader. Institutional transformation in Venezuela, if it occurs, will be a process measured in years, not weeks.

6.2 Implications for the Tren de Aragua: The Monster Without Its Incubator

The central operational question for U.S. law enforcement and security agencies is this: what does the fall of the regime that incubated the Tren de Aragua mean for the organization itself? The answer is complex and must resist the temptation of simplified optimism.

On one hand, the dismantling of the system that protected and facilitated the organization from within Venezuela eliminates one of its key strategic assets: the jurisdictional immunity of origin. If Venezuela under a transitional government cooperates with international law enforcement agencies — opening its criminal records databases, extraditing identified leaders, sharing intelligence on the organization's networks — the jurisdictional arbitrage that gave the Tren de Aragua its structural advantage suffers a foundational blow. The information gap that has prevented U.S. agencies from verifying the criminal histories of Venezuelan nationals can, for the first time in two decades, potentially be closed.

On the other hand, the Tren de Aragua is no longer the centralized organization that emerged from Tocorón. Since the September 2023 raid — which permitted the leadership's escape — the organization has operated under a decentralized franchise model that makes it inherently more resilient against disruptions in its country of origin. Cells in Colombia, Peru, Chile, Mexico, and the United States operate with significant autonomy. Nino Guerrero, whose whereabouts remain unknown as of publication, continues to be sought by the FBI with a reward exceeding $25 million. An organization of this architectural type does not collapse simply because the political environment of its founding country changes.

⚠ Strategic Warning for U.S. Law Enforcement and Security Agencies

> The most operationally dangerous assumption any U.S. security agency can make in the current environment is that Maduro's capture equals the dismantling of the Tren de Aragua. The organization has demonstrated remarkable resilience against disruptions far more severe than the political transition of its country of origin. Its cells on American soil will continue operating under the franchise model. Moreover, political uncertainty in Venezuela may generate new migration waves that the organization — with its established infrastructure for exploiting migration flows — is perfectly positioned to exploit. The window for intelligence cooperation with a transitional Venezuelan government is real and potentially decisive; it should be exploited urgently and strategically.

6.3 The Historic Opportunity: What Is Now Possible

The unfamiliar landscape also opens possibilities that were unthinkable while Maduro controlled the Venezuelan state apparatus. If the transitional government cooperates — and there are early indications of political will in that direction — it becomes possible for the first time in two decades to access Venezuelan penitentiary system records, criminal background databases, communications intelligence on the organization's networks, and documentary evidence establishing the identity of its members across multiple decades of criminal activity.

This is precisely the strategic opportunity that the following chapters — and the concrete proposal in Chapter Ten — are designed to address. Access to the Venezuelan judicial system's institutional knowledge, actors, procedures, and codes represents a bridge between the transitional Venezuelan state and the federal agencies that urgently need what that system can provide: verified intelligence on the criminal backgrounds of Venezuelan nationals on American soil.

The Venezuelan Criminal Records Verification Program — detailed in Chapter Ten — is not a theoretical policy recommendation. It is a concrete operational capability, resting on specific institutional knowledge and professional networks, that can begin contributing to U.S. security outcomes within months of authorization. The window of institutional cooperation with transitional Venezuela will not remain open indefinitely. The time to act is now.

VII. Timeline: Venezuela, the Tren de Aragua, and the Institutional Collapse

The following timeline summarizes the key moments of the process described in this chapter:

1999 Venezuela's New Constitution

The Chavista constitution concentrates executive power and begins the systematic Co-optation of the judiciary, Public Ministry, and security forces. The institutional architecture that will enable the criminal capture of the state is put in place.

2008–2012 El Aissami as Interior Minister

Tareck El Aissami oversees the Venezuelan penitentiary system during the institutionalization of the pranato. The "prison peace" model cedes effective control of prisons to pran leaders, creating the governance structure that will produce the Tren de Aragua.

2011 El Rodeo Riots and Creation of Ministry of Penitentiary Services

The 27-day El Rodeo prison siege exposes the state's loss of control over its own correctional facilities. The new Ministry of Penitentiary Services formalizes the pran system as a quasi-official governance instrument.

2012–2017 El Aissami as Governor of Aragua State

The architect of the pranato governs the state where Tocorón prison is located. Violence surges. Under Niño Guerrero's leadership, Tocorón is systematically converted into the Tren de Aragua's operational headquarters.

2013 Niño Guerrero Returns to Tocorón

Hector Rusthenford Guerrero Flores returns to Tocorón to serve a sentence for the murder of a police officer. He reorganizes and scales the criminal band from within the prison's walls.

2015–2019 The Great Venezuelan Migration Begins

Economic collapse under Maduro triggers the Venezuelan exodus. By 2019, over 4 million Venezuelans have left the country. The Tren de Aragua begins following the migration routes, establishing its transnational logistics network.

2017 El Aissami Named Vice President; U.S. Treasury Sanctions Him

Maduro appoints El Aissami as Executive Vice President. Within weeks, the U.S. Treasury designates him a narcotics trafficker. Maduro keeps him in government for over a year after the designation.

2020 First U.S. Federal Indictment Against Maduro

The DOJ presents the first federal indictment against Maduro and senior Venezuelan officials for narco-terrorism. The U.S. announces a $15 million reward for information leading to his arrest.

February 2024 Assassination of Ronald Ojeda in Chile

Dissident Venezuelan Lieutenant Ronald Ojeda is abducted and murdered in Santiago, Chile, by Tren de Aragua members with documented ties to the Maduro regime — the most extensively documented case of state-directed transnational criminal repression in the hemisphere.

September 2023 Tocorón Raid

11,000 Venezuelan soldiers storm Tocorón. The gang leadership — reportedly warned — escapes. Investigators find swimming pools, a zoo, a nightclub, restaurants, and military-grade weapons. The Tren de Aragua's departure from Tocorón accelerates its decentralized global expansion.

January–February 2025 U.S. Designates Tren de Aragua as Foreign Terrorist Organization

Trump signs Executive Order 14157 on January 20. Secretary Rubio formally designates the Tren de Aragua as an FTO on February 20 (Federal Register FR Doc. 2025-02873), placing it in the same legal category as al-Qaeda and ISIS.

January 3, 2026 Capture of Maduro: Operation Absolute Resolve

U.S. special forces capture Nicolas Maduro and Cilia Flores in Caracas. The same day, the Southern District of New York unseals a superseding indictment naming Niño Guerrero of the Tren de Aragua as a co-defendant of Maduro. The indictment charges narco-terrorism conspiracy, cocaine importation, and weapons offenses.

January 5, 2026 First Court Appearance in Manhattan

Maduro and Flores plead not guilty before Judge Hellerstein at the Moynihan Courthouse. Maduro declares himself a "prisoner of war." His attorney signals extensive pretrial litigation on immunity and the legality of the capture operation.

January–March 2026 Venezuela in Transition

Acting President Delcy Rodriguez oversees the release of 621 confirmed political prisoners. The UN Fact-Finding Mission warns that repressive state structures remain intact. Eighty-seven new politically motivated arrests are documented. The institutional transformation of Venezuela — and its implications for the Tren de Aragua's operational environment — is ongoing.

VIII. Chapter Summary: What Venezuela's History Teaches

The story this chapter has narrated is not a story of individual evil, though there are individuals who made profoundly destructive choices. It is a story of how institutional systems degenerate, how crime fills the vacuums left by a retreating state, and how, once that degradation reaches a certain threshold, its products — like the Tren de Aragua — acquire a life of their own and become independent of the regime that incubated them.

Three fundamental lessons emerge from this history for U.S. security professionals and policymakers:

■ **Lesson One: Origin Determines Architecture**

The Tren de Aragua is not simply a gang that grew. It is an organization shaped by the Venezuelan penitentiary experience: its hierarchy, codes, loyalty rituals, and control mechanisms reflect the prison culture that produced it. Understanding that origin is understanding the organization. Field agents who can recognize pranato-derived organizational logic — the tren/carro structure, the pran authority model, the vacuna revenue mechanism — are equipped to identify organizational affiliation even in the absence of explicit membership documentation.

■ Lesson Two: State Complicity Does Not Disappear with the State

Although the Maduro regime has fallen, the network of actors who facilitated and benefited from the Tren de Aragua's existence — corrupt officials, bribed police, politically connected figures — continues to exist inside and outside Venezuela. Political transition does not automatically equal institutional decontamination. U.S. agencies engaging with transitional Venezuelan authorities must apply the same rigorous vetting standards they would apply to any partner emerging from an environment of systemic institutional corruption.

■ Lesson Three: The New Opportunity Must Be Seized Urgently

For the first time in two decades, genuine access to Venezuelan criminal records, penitentiary intelligence, and institutional cooperation is potentially available. That window — which can close rapidly if the political transition stalls or new actors capture the institutions — must be exploited with urgency and with the expertise of those who understand the Venezuelan system from within. This is the subject of the concrete proposals in Chapter Ten.

Chapter Three turns to the operational core: the internal anatomy of the Tren de Aragua itself. Its leadership structure, communication systems, criminal portfolio, identification markers, and behavioral patterns. The analytical intelligence in Chapter Three is what transforms the historical understanding built in Chapters One and Two into actionable field knowledge — the kind that equips an FBI task force, a DEA analyst, a border security agent, or an immigration judge with the specific, granular understanding of this organization that no general report can provide.

— END OF CHAPTER TWO —

CHAPTER THREE

Anatomy of the Organization

Internal structure, hierarchy, lexicon, criminal operations, and identification indicators

Introductory Note: Why This Chapter Matters in the Field

The previous chapters provided the historical and institutional context of the Tren de Aragua. This chapter is different in purpose: it is designed to be useful in the field. Its primary audience is FBI, DEA, ICE, and HSI agents who encounter the organization's members or cells in their investigations; federal prosecutors who need to understand criminal enterprise structure to build RICO cases; immigration judges who must evaluate alleged affiliations; and intelligence analysts who need to distinguish between genuine members, imitators, and victims who have been erroneously categorized as perpetrators.

A critical warning from the outset: identifying individuals as Tren de Aragua members requires holistic analysis that goes far beyond superficial visual indicators. The painful experience of the March 2025 deportations — in which individuals were sent to CECOT in El Salvador-based on tattoo evaluations that proved entirely unrelated to the organization — illustrates the devastating consequences of superficial identification. The organization genuinely does not require its members to display specific identifying tattoos. This chapter provides the correct criteria.

I. The Organizational Model: The Criminal Franchise

1.1 Why the Tren de Aragua Is Not an Ordinary Gang

The most frequent conceptual error in analyzing the Tren de Aragua is treating it as an enlarged street gang — a Venezuelan version of MS-13 or the Crips. That categorization, while producing comprehensible headlines, distorts analysis and leads to misguided interdiction strategies. The Tren de Aragua is different from conventional street gangs across three dimensions: its institutional origin, its organizational architecture, and its expansion methodology.

In terms of origin, the Tren de Aragua did not emerge from the streets: it emerged from the institutions of the Venezuelan state — specifically, the penitentiary institution. That means its organizational DNA incorporates the governance patterns, control mechanisms, and authority structures that the pranes developed to administer complex institutions — not simply to survive in the street crime marketplace. The difference between a gang that controls a corner and an organization that administered a 1,600-inmate prison with its own courts, tax system, and criminal foreign policy is the difference between a tactical operation and a strategic enterprise.

In terms of architecture, the Tren de Aragua does not replicate the rigid, centralized hierarchical structure of classical Colombian or Mexican cartels. It has developed what organizational criminologists call a "hierarchical network structure": hierarchical at the apex (central leadership with ultimate authority) but reticular in execution (semi-autonomous cells that operate with local adaptation). This model combines the strategic coherence of hierarchy with the operational resilience of the network, producing an organization that is extraordinarily difficult to dismantle through conventional leadership-decapitation techniques.

1.2 The Tren-Carro Structure: The Basic Organizational Unit

The fundamental organizational unit of the Tren de Aragua is the tren-carro duality, operating at two distinct hierarchical levels:

- **The Tren (Train)**

A "tren" is a mid-level organizational unit: a set of criminal operators under shared leadership, with assigned territory, specific criminal portfolio, and responsibility for reporting upward in the hierarchy. In the original prison context, a tren controlled a cell block or prison sector. In the current transnational context, a tren may control a neighborhood, a trafficking zone, a border crossing, or a sexual exploitation operation. The tren leader is called the "train leader" or simply referenced by name or alias.

- **The Carro (Car)**

  A "carro" is the minimum operational unit: a cell of three to fifteen individuals specialized in a specific criminal activity. The carro operates with considerable tactical autonomy, adapting its methods to the local conditions of the criminal market in which it operates. The "carro" as a concept is the unit most likely to be encountered in field investigations: when a Tren de Aragua operation is intercepted, investigators are typically disrupting a carro, not the complete tren.

From a criminal intelligence perspective, this architecture has direct implications for investigative strategy. A successful operation against a carro — without understanding of the tren that houses it and the network of parallel carros — is a tactical success that rarely translates into strategic impact on the organization. The RICO model, applied to the Tren de Aragua, requires precisely this level of structural analysis: demonstrating the pattern of racketeering activity that links individual cells within the broader criminal enterprise.

1.3 The Leadership Hierarchy

The Tren de Aragua's leadership structure operates across four levels, each with distinct functions, responsibilities, and vulnerabilities to law enforcement:

- **Level 1: The Pran / Supreme Leader**

    Hector "Nino Guerrero" Rusthenford Guerrero Flores occupies this role. The supreme leader establishes the organization's strategic direction, authorizes large-scale operations, adjudicates disputes between lower-level leaders, and maintains control of the organization's central financial assets. Since the Tocorón raid of September 2023, Nino Guerrero has operated from an unknown location. The FBI lists him among its most wanted fugitives with a reward exceeding $25 million. The Departments of Treasury and State have designated him with SDNT (Specially Designated Narcotics Trafficker) status.

- **Level 2: Regional Lieutenants**

    Regional lieutenants are the organization's operational executives: they administer multiple trenes within a geographic region, coordinate between cells, manage the upward financial flow to supreme leadership, and have authority to allow mid-level operations. They are the individuals who connect strategic direction with tactical execution. Their capture or neutralization has the greatest operational impact on the organization — greater, in the short term, even than the supreme leader's.

- **Level 3: Tren Leaders**

  They administer a specific operational unit, supervise multiple carros, maintain internal discipline within their tren, execute regional-level directives, and report upward. They are the primary point of contact for operational cells and, therefore, the individuals with the greatest knowledge of the organization's daily operations. They are also, many times, the most valuable subjects for cooperator development.

- **Level 4: Carro Members**

  These are field operators: the individuals who execute daily criminal activities of extortion, trafficking, contract killing, and territorial control. They have limited knowledge of the organization's global structure — they know their carro, their tren leader, and their immediate operational peers. This compartmentalization of knowledge is deliberate and reduces the organization's vulnerability to cooperators who can only provide information about their own level of the hierarchy.

II. The Organization's Lexicon: Field Reference Guide

The Tren de Aragua's language is a coded system that simultaneously fulfills multiple criminological functions: it establishes group identity, obscures communication content from outside observers, creates barriers to organizational entry (only those who know the code belong), and perpetuates the band's institutional culture as it expands geographically. For the agent or analyst working Tren de Aragua cases, mastery of this lexicon is a directly applicable investigative tool.

The following table presents the most operationally relevant terms of the Tren de Aragua, with their meaning and relevance for law enforcement work:

Term	Operational meaning	Relevance for agents
Pran	De facto leader of the organization or a level of its hierarchy. From the acronym "Preso Rematado Asesino Nato" (natural-born killer prisoner). Maximum level of authority within the band.	*When a suspect references "el pran" in intercepted communications, they are referring to the leader of their unit or the entire organization.*
Tren	Mid-level organizational unit. Originally referred to the group of inmates controlling a prison section.	*Membership in a specific "tren" identifies organizational affiliation and territorial responsibility.*
Carro	Minimum operational cell. Group of 3-15 individuals	*Most likely unit to be encountered in field*

Term	Description	Indicator
	specialized in a specific criminal activity.	*investigations. Identifying the "carro" allows mapping of the superior structure.*
Vacuna	Periodic extortion payment demanded from businesses, residents, and other subjects in controlled territory. Analogous to the "Pizzo" of the Italian Cosa Nostra.	*Pattern of regular payments to unknown third parties is a powerful indicator of vacuna victimization. Victims rarely report because of fear of retaliation.*
Convive	Organization member who has completed "initiation" and holds full status within the structure. Equivalent to the Italian Mafia's "made man."	*The "convive" status confers protection and privileges within the organization. It is an indicator of established affiliation.*
La Causa	Internal quota system that members pay to the superior hierarchy. In Tocorón, generated approximately $3.5M annually.	*Regular payment flows from multiple individuals to the same account or person are indicators of "causa" in laundering operations.*
Plazas	Territorial control zones where the organization has established stable criminal operations. Control of a "plaza" is equivalent to the original prison territorial control.	*Identifying the distribution of "plazas" in a city allows mapping of the organization's territorial footprint and expansion routes.*

Gota a gota	Usurious loan system with extreme interest rates (typically 20-50% monthly), targeting low-income immigrant communities. Named for the frequency of payments falling "drop by drop."	*Gota a gota operations leave financial traces in multiple payment recipient accounts. The pattern of frequent small transfers from multiple senders is a red flag.*
Sicariato	Contract murder service. One of the organization's primary revenue sources and most important control instrument.	*When TdA operates as a "service provider" for other local criminal organizations, contract killing is frequently the contracted service.*
Limpiar	To execute a person by organizational order. May refer to disloyal members, witnesses, resistant victims, or rivals.	*In intercepted communications, "limpiar" or "hacer la limpieza" is coded language for ordering or confirming a murder.*
Los Guerreros / Los Sanos	Designations for specialized subgroups. "Los Guerreros" are the armed wing; "Los Sanos" are operators in communities not yet incarcerated.	*These subgroup designations may appear in tattoos, communications, or witness statements and help identify the individual's organizational role.*
Trocha	Unofficial informal border crossing used for irregular migration. Trochas are the organization's primary	*A suspect's knowledge of specific trochas is a significant*

	logistics routes for moving people, weapons, and drugs.	*indicator of involvement in human trafficking or smuggling.*

2.1 Encrypted Communications: The Emoji System

One of the most striking findings of Tren de Aragua investigations — and one of the most relevant for communications intelligence work — is the systematic use of emoji sequences as operational communication code. Rather than transmitting orders in text that could easily be interpreted by investigators, the organization developed a system in which specific emoji sequences posted in WhatsApp, Instagram, and Telegram temporary status updates encode operational orders: from delivery confirmations to violence instructions.

This communication system is criminologically sophisticated for several reasons. First, the content — commonly used emojis — does not trigger conventional communications surveillance filters. Second, WhatsApp and Snapchat "status" features automatically disappear within 24 hours, leaving minimal digital trace. Third, the code's meaning varies by cell and by period, making decoding without an internal informant extremely difficult.

🔍 **FIELD NOTE FOR AGENTS**

Interception of emoji communications on social media requires judicial authorization for real-time capture, given that temporary status updates disappear within 24 hours. When emoji communication is identified in seized devices, the temporal context (send time, relationship to contemporaneous events) is crucial for decoding. The use of cooperating informants with knowledge of the specific cell's code is frequently the only effective interpretation pathway.

III. The Criminal Portfolio: Diversification and Evolution

One of the most distinctive organizational characteristics of the Tren de Aragua — and the one that most confuses security agencies accustomed to the specializations of classical cartels — is its extraordinarily diversified criminal portfolio. The Tren de Aragua is not a narco-cartel, though it traffics drugs. It is not a human trafficking organization, though it traffics humans. It is not an extortion ring, though it systematically extorts. It is, in the most precise criminological sense, a "multi-crime" enterprise: an organization that has developed the capacity to operate profitably across multiple criminal markets simultaneously.

This diversification is not accidental: it is an adaptive strategy that maximizes revenue, distributes legal risk across multiple criminal typifications, and allows the organization to operate in environments where some activities are more difficult to execute than others. When law enforcement pressure on drug trafficking increases in a jurisdiction, the organization can redirect resources toward extortion or human trafficking. When the trafficking market saturates, it can expand the gota a gota. This portfolio approach to organized crime is a methodological innovation that security agencies are still developing responses to counter.

3.1 Human Trafficking and Sexual Exploitation

Human trafficking for sexual exploitation is, alongside extortion, the Tren de Aragua's foundational crime in its transnational phase. The organization exploits the structural vulnerability of Venezuelan migrant women in three distinct ways: fraudulent recruitment (overseas job offers that turn out to be exploitation networks), forced indebtedness (charging "travel debts" that become control mechanisms), and direct coercion through threats to family members remaining in Venezuela.

From the perspective of U.S. federal law enforcement, these facts make up offenses under the Trafficking Victims Protection Act (TVPA, 18 U.S.C. §

1591 et seq.), with maximum penalties of life imprisonment when victims are minors or when force, fraud, or coercion is employed. The transnational nature of the operation also activates the federal international trafficking statute (18 U.S.C. § 1591(a)(2)), extending jurisdiction to recruitment and transport operations conducted outside the United States.

🔍 OPERATIONAL TRAFFICKING INDICATORS

Tren de Aragua victims rarely self-identify as such. Field indicators include: multiple Venezuelan women at the same address with restricted freedom of movement; identity documents held by third parties; evidence of "debt" payments to a single recipient; presence of a male "handler" in interviews who responds on behalf of victims; visible fear when Venezuelan authorities are mentioned or when family contact is offered; and pattern of moving between multiple addresses in short periods. Under TVPA's federal victim-centered approach, interviewing potential victims in a safe environment separated from suspected handlers is a threshold requirement.

3.2 Extortion: The Vacuna and Territorial Control

Extortion — the "vacuna" in the organization's language — is the most stable and predictable revenue mechanism of the Tren de Aragua. Unlike drug trafficking, which requires product logistics, or human trafficking, which requires constant victim recruitment, extortion is a recurring revenue stream that flows automatically once territorial control is established. It is the criminal equivalent of passive income.

The vacuna's operational scheme follows an easily recognizable pattern: initial contact with the business owner or residential target; presentation of the "protection offer" (often without explicitly naming the organization); establishment of a periodic amount (weekly or monthly) calibrated to the perceived payment capacity of the target; and demonstrative consequences for non-payers — violence against the person, property destruction, or threats against family members. Terror is not a byproduct of extortion: it is its primary maintenance instrument.

Venezuelan diaspora communities in the United States are particularly vulnerable targets because: (a) migrants in irregular status are reluctant to contact authorities; (b) threats against family members remaining in Venezuela are credible and executable; and (c) the extortionist's cultural knowledge of the victim — including family location, immigration status, and life patterns — provides coercive leverage that is unavailable to criminal organizations without this background knowledge.

🔍 EVIDENCE COLLECTION IN VACUNA CASES

TdA extortion frequently leaves no documentary trace, as payments are cash-based and victims avoid authorities.

The most effective collection techniques include: surveillance cameras in affected businesses; telephone records of targets (with authorization); confidential interviews through trusted community organizations; cooperating witnesses with protection; and analysis of business closure patterns in areas of high Venezuelan concentration. Correlation between business closures and TdA cell arrival in a neighborhood is a documented pattern in Chicago, Miami, New York, and Houston. Under federal extortion statutes (18 U.S.C. § 1951 — the Hobbs Act), extortion affecting interstate commerce falls within federal jurisdiction even without an explicit interstate commerce nexus.

3.3 Drug Trafficking: The Tren de Aragua's Role in the Drug Market

The Tren de Aragua's relationship with drug trafficking is more complex and nuanced than its frequent conflation with major cartels in public discourse suggests. The organization is not, in its origin or its primary business model, a narco-cartel. However, it has integrated drug trafficking — particularly retail-level distribution and transit logistics — into its criminal portfolio as it has established territorial control across different countries.

The documented pattern shows that the Tren de Aragua operates in drug trafficking primarily in three modalities: as a "escort" and logistics service provider for other cartels operating in its territories; as a retail drug distributor in the residential areas where it has established territorial control; and as an intermediary in cocaine transit through Venezuela and its migration routes toward Central America and the United States. The January 3, 2026 indictment against Maduro explicitly includes Nino Guerrero as an operator of "escort services for cocaine shipments and control of coastal storage facilities."

3.4 The Gota a Gota: Usurious Lending as a Control Instrument

The loan system known as "gota a gota" — named for the frequency of payments falling "drop by drop" on the borrower — is one of the most devastating criminal instruments deployed against immigrant communities and one of the least visible to authorities. The scheme operates as follows: a person in financial need receives a cash loan, typically without formal documentation, at an interest rate that can range from 20% to 100% monthly. The repayment scheme requires daily or weekly payments. The mathematical impossibility of settling the debt converts the borrower into a permanent debtor who can be mobilized for criminal activities, labor-exploited, or subjected to extortion under threat of violence against themselves or their family members.

The gota a gota was imported by the Tren de Aragua from Colombian criminal practices and adapted to

Venezuelan diaspora communities. It constitutes a federal offense under extortion and predatory lending statutes (18 U.S.C. §§ 891-894), but its prosecution is systematically complicated by victims' reluctance to report, their frequent irregular immigration status, and the absence of written documentation of the original loan.

3.5 Contract Killing: Murder as a Service and as Control

Contract killing — sicariato — serves two distinct functions within the Tren de Aragua's business model. As an external service, the organization offers executions to other criminal bands, rival organizations, and in some documented cases, corrupt public officials or regimes requiring "problem elimination" without traceable links. The price of a Tren de Aragua contract killing has been documented in ranges from $3,000 to $50,000 depending on the target's profile and operation complexity.

As an internal control instrument, contract killing is the ultimate organizational enforcement mechanism: it eliminates disloyal members, potential witnesses, resistant victims, and rivals who challenge the band's territorial control. The extreme and visible nature of violence exercised by TdA contract killers — including mutilations, torture, and beheadings that are recorded and distributed on social media — is not a deviation from their method: it is a central part of it. Terror is the product, and the distribution of extreme violence imagery on TikTok and WhatsApp is the marketing strategy for that product.

IV. Terror as Strategic Instrument: Digital Warfare

4.1 TikTok as a Psychological Weapon

One of the Tren de Aragua's most important operational innovations — and the one that most clearly positions it as a Fourth Wave criminal organization — is its strategic use of social media platforms as instruments of psychological warfare and criminal brand management. This use goes far beyond recruitment or internal communication: it is a deliberate strategy for producing fear at mass scale.

On TikTok, Instagram, and YouTube, band members and supporters publish videos displaying weapons arsenals, large quantities of cash, executions by contract killers, and testimonials of the organization's capacity to commit violence with impunity. Academic research by Erazo-Patino and collaborators (2025) on the TdA's "digital narrative" on TikTok documents deliberate discursive policies that reflect the organization's structure, operativity, and impact on the digital imagination. These narratives simultaneously serve three functions: intimidating potential victims, recruiting members who aspire to the status the band projects, and discouraging witness cooperation with authorities.

SOCIAL MEDIA INTELLIGENCE

Public accounts associated with TdA on TikTok and Instagram are a significant open-source intelligence (OSINT) source. Usage patterns — posting schedules, undeleted geolocations, social network connections between accounts, identifiable objects in images — have allowed investigators to identify locations, map networks, and develop investigative targets. Collaboration with cyber-intelligence units for systematic monitoring of associated accounts is an investigative capability that every unit working TdA cases should develop. Under 18 U.S.C. § 2703 and related electronic surveillance authorities, properly allowed collection of social media data constitutes admissible evidence in federal prosecutions.

V. Member Identification: Correct Criteria and Common Errors

5.1 The Problem with Tattoo-Based Identification

No area of operational intelligence on the Tren de Aragua has been more harmfully misinterpreted than that relating to tattoos. The mass deportations of March 2025 — in which dozens of Venezuelans were sent to El Salvador's CECOT prison based on criteria that included tattoo evaluation — illustrated in devastating fashion the practical consequences of this misinterpretation. A gay tattoo artist who had fled Venezuela due to persecution for his sexual orientation and political beliefs was deported to CECOT because his tattoos — which said "Mom" and "Dad" on his wrists — were interpreted as indicators of gang affiliation.

The criminological reality is straightforward: the Tren de Aragua does NOT mandate or promote a standardized system of affiliation tattoos. Unlike Central American maras — especially MS-13, which has relatively standardized though declining tattoo systems — the Tren de Aragua emerged from a Venezuelan prison culture where tattoos are broad cultural expressions, influenced by reggaeton music, urban culture, and youth aesthetics, and not primarily criminal affiliation markers. FBI investigators, DEA researchers, and specialized academic organizations agree on this point: identification by isolated tattoos, without correlation with other factors, lacks solid methodological foundation for the Tren de Aragua.

⚠ CRITICAL WARNING: METHODOLOGICAL IDENTIFICATION ERROR

The presence of tattoos on a Venezuelan individual is NOT, by itself, a reliable indicator of Tren de Aragua affiliation. Identification that leads to legal consequences — including designation as a member for deportation, indictment, or detention — must be based on multiple correlated criteria, including corroborated criminal intelligence, behavioral patterns, prior records, and evidence of participation in the organization's activities. One-dimensional identification based on physical appearance is legally vulnerable, ethically problematic, and operationally counterproductive. Federal courts reviewing deportation determinations under the AEA and INA will scrutinize identification methodology. Faulty identification procedures will generate civil liability exposure for agencies.

5.2 Evidence-Based Identification Criteria

Evidence-grounded identification of Tren de Aragua members — the kind that can sustain a federal indictment, an immigration determination, or a terrorist organization membership designation — requires correlation of multiple indicators within a holistic analysis. The following criteria, grouped by category, constitute the recommended methodological standard:

■ **Corroborated Intelligence Criteria**
Identification by informants with direct knowledge of the organization; inclusion in criminal intelligence databases with documented sources; documented association with

previously identified members; appearance in intercepted communications in an organizational context; and identification by foreign authorities in international criminal cooperation. Under the federal standards applicable to material support prosecutions (18 U.S.C. § 2339B), the evidentiary burden requires knowing and intentional provision of support to a designated FTO — requiring precisely this level of corroborated intelligence.

- **Behavioral and Pattern Criteria**

  Documented participation in activities characteristic of TdA operations (extortion of Venezuelan communities, gota a gota operations, human trafficking); exercise of territorial control over diaspora concentration areas; use of Venezuelan prison lexicon in documented communications; stable association pattern with identified criminal structure; and demonstrated knowledge of organizational protocols such as the vacuna collection system or carro structure.

- **Documentary Criteria**

  Verifiable criminal records in Venezuela for offenses characteristic of the organization; Venezuelan penitentiary records establishing incarceration at Tocorón or other TdA-controlled facilities during relevant periods; identity records establishing connections to known criminal locations and networks. This is the category where the Venezuelan Criminal Records Verification Program provides unique operational value: accessing these records, previously unavailable to U.S. agencies due to

Venezuelan state non-cooperation, can now potentially be pursued through a transitional Venezuelan government.

■ Visual Indicators (as complementary elements ONLY, NEVER in isolation)

The following visual elements may be complementary indicators when correlated with the above criteria: use of the "pran" aesthetic (fitted clothing of recognized brands, thick gold chains, flat-brim caps); documented body language and gestural symbolism in criminal contexts; and — with extreme caution and only as a complementary indicator — tattoos whose content, context, and the bearer's own acknowledgment of their meaning correlate with organizational affiliation.

5.3 The Imitator Problem

A significant complicating factor for identification is the proliferation of "imitators" — individuals and criminal groups who use the Tren de Aragua name and aesthetic without genuine organizational affiliation. This phenomenon, documented in multiple Latin American countries and in Venezuelan communities in the United States, occurs because the "Tren de Aragua" brand has intimidatory value that opportunistic criminals seek to leverage. The terror aesthetic the organization has deliberately cultivated through social media creates a brand asset that can be exploited by those without genuine affiliation.

For law enforcement, the distinction between genuine TdA members and imitators is operationally crucial: an imitator cannot provide intelligence on the real organization's structure; prosecution of imitators as TdA members produces arrest statistics that overestimate the band's actual reach; and differentiation allows focusing investigative resources on the highest-value strategic targets. The RICO enterprise theory applied to TdA requires demonstrating actual membership in and participation in the affairs of the criminal enterprise — a standard that imitators cannot satisfy, and which protects legitimate prosecution from legal challenge.

VI. The Expansion Model on American Soil

6.1 Documented Presence in the United States

The Tren de Aragua's presence in the United States is a documented fact, though its scale and degree of organization have been subject to debate among security analysts. From January through December 2025, the Department of Justice indicted over 260 TdA members across five federal districts: Colorado, Nebraska, New Mexico, the Southern District of New York, and the Southern District of Texas. Charges include RICO conspiracy, extortion, murder, human trafficking, money laundering, and drug distribution.

Cities with documentation of TdA operations on American soil include — without constituting an exhaustive list — New York (particularly the Bronx and Queens), Miami, Houston, Aurora (Colorado), Chicago, Las Vegas, and Los Angeles. In all these jurisdictions, the operational pattern follows the three-phase expansion model: initial establishment in communities of high Venezuelan migrant concentration, followed by community extortion, and eventually diversification toward other criminal markets.

6.2 The Aurora, Colorado Case: A Study in Operational Pattern

No American city illustrates the Tren de Aragua's expansion cycle more clearly than Aurora, Colorado. In 2024, videos circulating on social media appeared to show armed individuals taking control of low-cost apartment complexes in the city, described as a TdA "takeover" of residential properties. The media coverage generated immediate national attention and was prominently referenced in the 2024 presidential campaign.

Subsequent criminological analysis — including FBI and Aurora Police Department investigations — revealed a more nuanced picture than the initial narrative. There were genuine TdA operations in certain buildings:

extortion of Venezuelan residents, drug trafficking control in some complexes, and human trafficking activity. However, the description of a coordinated "takeover" of the city was a pre-election period exaggeration. The Aurora case illustrates both the reality of TdA presence and the risk of political overdimensionalization of that presence — both tendencies damaging to the formulation of precise security responses.

🔍 LESSON FROM THE AURORA CASE

Effective response to the TdA in American communities requires distinguishing between the real threat — which is serious and requires significant investigative resources — and the perceived threat, which can be amplified by media panic, political considerations, and the organization's own terror-brand strategy. Data-based threat assessments — rather than media coverage or political rhetoric — are essential for efficient allocation of security resources. This distinction is not academic: the over-identification of TdA membership in Aurora and elsewhere generated civil rights litigation, undermined community trust essential for witness cooperation, and diverted investigative resources from genuine organizational targets.

VII. Chapter Operational Summary

This chapter has built the operational profile of the Tren de Aragua with the granularity level necessary for practical field application. The key points for the security professional are:

■ **On Structure**

The tren-carro-pran architecture is the fundamental organizational framework. Investigations must map the complete structure, not limit themselves to the immediate cell. The RICO model is the most appropriate legal instrument for prosecuting this structure as a criminal enterprise. Each indictment should be constructed to show the pattern of racketeering connecting individual cells within the broader enterprise.

■ **On Lexicon**

Mastery of TdA's operational lexicon — especially in intercepted communications — multiplies the probative value of captured conversations. The terminology table in this chapter is a quick-reference field tool. Foreign language communications in Venezuelan prison argot should be translated by interpreters specifically familiar with this subculture, not just general Spanish speakers.

■ **On the Criminal Portfolio**

TdA operates a "multi-crime" portfolio including extortion, trafficking, drug distribution, gota a gota, contract killing, and laundering. Investigations limited to a single charge typification frequently underestimate the breadth and value of the organization's criminal activity. Multi-charge indictments that capture the full portfolio better represent the criminal enterprise and provide stronger leverage for cooperation development.

■ On Identification

Tattoo-based identification in isolation is methodologically unsustainable and legally vulnerable. The correct standard requires correlation of multiple criteria: corroborated intelligence, behavioral patterns, documentary records, and — only as a complementary element — visual indicators. Distinguishing between genuine members and imitators is an operational and legal priority. Faulty identification method generates civil rights litigation and undermines prosecution integrity.

Chapter Four focuses on the specific American scenario: the Tren de Aragua threat on U.S. soil, the most relevant federal cases, the specific challenges for American law enforcement agencies, and the intelligence gaps that access to Venezuelan records can close. It also examines how the January 3, 2026 indictment of Maduro reshapes the operational environment for every agency working TdA cases in the United States.

IDENTIFICATION GUIDE: TATTOOS AND SYMBOLS

SECTION A — INCORRECT IDENTIFICATION: COMMON TATTOOS THAT DO NOT INDICATE TdA AFFILIATION

The following tattoos have been erroneously used as identification criteria. Their presence alone has NO evidentiary value for TdA affiliation.

TABLE 1 — INCORRECT IDENTIFICATION INDICATORS		
LABEL	TATTOO / SYMBOL	WHY IT IS NOT AN INDICATOR
Documented Error (Deportations 2025)	**"Mom" / "Dad" on wrists**	Common family tattoos in Venezuelan culture. A gay tattoo artist was deported to CECOT for this. NO affiliation indicator.
Frequent Misinterpretation	**Roses / Ornamental Flowers**	Decorative tattoo common in Latin urban aesthetics, influenced by reggaeton culture. Not a TdA symbol.
Context Required	**Crowns / Watches / Dice**	"Trap" and urban Venezuelan aesthetic elements. Isolated presence does not establish affiliation.
Cultural Aesthetic	**Tears / Dots on Face**	Associated with crime culture in the U.S., but common in Venezuelan art and popular culture. Not TdA-specific.
Totally Neutral	**Religious Symbols / Crosses / Rosaries**	Extremely common in Venezuelan Catholic culture. No indicative value for criminal affiliation.

SECTION B — CORRECT METHODOLOGICAL STANDARD

Evidence-based identification requires correlation of MULTIPLE criteria in a holistic analysis. Visual indicators are ONLY complementary elements and NEVER sufficient on their own.

TABLE 2 — CORRECT METHODOLOGICAL STANDARD (Multi-Criteria)		
#	CRITERION	OPERATIONAL CONTENT
1	**Corroborated Intelligence**	Positive ID from informants with direct knowledge. Inclusion in criminal databases. Appearance in intercepted communications in organizational context.
2	**Behavioral and Pattern Criteria**	Documented participation in extortion of Venezuelan communities, gota a gota

#		
		operations, or trafficking. Stable association with identified criminal structure.
3	**Documentary Criteria**	Verifiable criminal records in Venezuela. Prison records at Tocorón or other TdA-controlled prisons (2013–2023). Identity documents with connections to known criminal networks.
4	**Visual Indicators (Complementary Only)**	"Pran" aesthetic: fitted brand-name clothing, thick gold chains, flat-brim caps. Body language and gestural symbology in documented criminal contexts. Tattoos ONLY as complementary indicators correlated with other criteria.
5	**Physical Property Marks (HIGH SPECIFICITY)**	State Dept. TIP Report (2025): TdA "marked women and girls behind ears to show ownership." This mark, combined with other indicators, is a HIGH-SPECIFICITY victim indicator — not membership.

SECTION C — HIGH-SPECIFICITY VISUAL INDICATORS (When Correlated)

These elements MAY have indicative value only when correlated with criteria from Section B above.

TABLE 3 — HIGH-SPECIFICITY INDICATORS (When Correlated)		
INDICATOR	**SPECIFICITY LEVEL**	**OPERATIONAL NOTES**
"Tren de Aragua" / "TdA" / "TA"	HIGH (in context)	Explicit name of the organization confirmed by carrier. Combined with corroborated intelligence, high ID value. Rare — the band does not require formal marks.
Stylized Locomotive / Train Image	MEDIUM-HIGH (in context)	When carrier explicitly associates with the band in declarations or communications. As an isolated element, insufficient. Requires carrier confirmation or intelligence.
"Los Guerreros" / "Los Sanos"	HIGH (with intelligence)	TdA subgroup designations. 'Los Guerreros' is the armed wing. Presence in tattoo, combined with intelligence, identifies the individual's organizational role.
Mark Behind Ear (women)	VICTIM INDICATOR	Documented by U.S. State Dept. as TdA 'property' marks in trafficking victims. HIGH diagnostic specificity for VICTIMIZATION, not membership.

SECTION D — WHY TdA DIFFERS FROM OTHER GANGS

TABLE 4 — KEY DIFFERENCE: TdA vs. MS-13 TATTOO SYSTEMS	
MS-13	**TREN DE ARAGUA (TdA)**

Historically standardized tattoo system (though declining)	**NO standardized tattoo affiliation system**
Agents trained to identify MS-13 can follow visual patterns	**Same method CANNOT be applied to TdA — different criminal culture**
Emerged from Central American gang culture with visual identity markers	Emerged from Venezuelan prison culture — tattoos are individual expressions influenced by reggaeton, urban culture, and youth aesthetics

CRITICAL WARNING FOR AGENTS AND INVESTIGATORS: Tattoo-based identification in isolation is methodologically indefensible and legally vulnerable for TdA. The correct standard requires correlation of multiple criteria. One-dimensional identification generated the deportation of innocent individuals to CECOT in 2025, with documented legal, diplomatic, and security costs. Federal courts reviewing AEA and INA determinations will scrutinize identification methodology. © 2026 Rolnar A. Sanabria Bernatte · LISE · CAGE: 157Z2

— END OF CHAPTER THREE —

CHAPTER FOUR

Human Trafficking: The Invisible Crime

How the Tren de Aragua recruits, transports, and exploits its victims from Venezuela to the United States

Warning and Purpose of This Chapter

This chapter contains material of serious gravity. It describes the recruitment, transport, control, and exploitation techniques used by the Tren de Aragua against its victims. It does so with a single, rational purpose: to equip security professionals, legislators, judges, attorneys, social workers, and the public with the knowledge needed to identify, document, prosecute, and — above all — prevent these crimes.

Trafficking victims are real people. They are not statistics. Every woman, every young person, every minor who appears in this chapter as a documented case or part of a pattern is a human being whose life was destroyed or profoundly altered by organized violence. This documentation is written with the respect and dignity those lives deserve, and with the determination that this knowledge serve to combat the system that victimized them.

Human trafficking committed by the Tren de Aragua is not a peripheral crime within its criminal portfolio: it is one of its foundational pillars — the activity that funded its first transnational expansion and that today generates recurring revenue in over fifteen countries. Understanding it fully means understanding the organization.

I. Human Trafficking as a Strategic Pillar of TdA

1.1 The Origin of the Model: Venezuela as Laboratory

Sexual exploitation of migrant women was not an activity the Tren de Aragua adopted late in its expansion. From a criminological perspective, it was one of its foundational business models: the first activity the organization systematically exported when it began following Venezuelan migration flows from 2017 onward. The U.S. Department of the Treasury, when sanctioning the Tren de Aragua in July 2024 as a Significant Transnational Criminal Organization, described this mechanism precisely: the organization "leverages its transnational networks to traffic people, especially migrant women and girls, across borders for sex trafficking and debt bondage. When victims seek to escape this exploitation, Tren de Aragua members often kill them and publicize their deaths as a threat to others."

Within Venezuela, before transnational expansion, the Tren de Aragua had already developed a sexual exploitation model within the territory controlled by the band. Hyperinflation, catastrophic unemployment, and the collapse of social services created a reservoir of women in situations of extreme vulnerability. The organization perfected its techniques of captation, control, and victim monetization within the Venezuelan context before scaling them to a continental level.

The most revealing data point about the centrality of trafficking in TdA's business model is that when the band expands to new territories, sexual exploitation is frequently the first activity it establishes — before drug trafficking, before contract killing, even before generalized extortion. It is the entry point into the local criminal market because it requires less initial capital, generates immediate income, and can be established rapidly by leveraging existing migration infrastructure.

1.2 The "Multadas": The Term That Defines the Victims

Within the Tren de Aragua's internal language, victims of sexual exploitation are called "multadas" — from the Spanish "multas" or "those who pay fines." The term is criminologically revealing: it converts the victim into a debtor, into someone who must pay a "fine" to the organization for having used its migration transit services, for having incurred accommodation debts, or simply for having been declared "property" of the band.

The December 2025 federal superseding indictment in the Southern District of New York against Nino Guerrero and Tren de Aragua leadership explicitly documents the use of this term: prosecutors describe how women were "smuggled from Venezuela into countries including Colombia, Peru, and the United States and forced into commercial sex work to repay debts, with compliance enforced through threats, assault, kidnapping, and murder." This indictment — which also charges Nino Guerrero with directing and supporting these acts — is the most complete available legal documentation of the "multadas" scheme as an organized criminal system.

⚠ **KEY LANGUAGE FOR AGENTS AND INVESTIGATORS**

When intercepted communications, victim testimonies, or cooperator statements contain the word "multada" or "la multa" regarding a woman, this is a high-value terminological indicator that credits the use of TdA's trafficking scheme. This coded language identifies both the victim and the control system to which she is subjected. It constitutes significant circumstantial evidence of organizational membership and criminal enterprise participation under RICO theory.

II. The Trafficking Cycle: The Four Phases.

Human trafficking perpetrated by the Tren de Aragua is not improvised activity. It follows a systematic, replicable four-phase cycle that has been documented by authorities across multiple countries and that operates with a consistency that reveals its institutional character — that is, its nature as a deliberate organizational system rather than the sum of individual behaviors.

Phase 1: Recruitment — The Deception Trap

The Tren de Aragua recruits victims primarily through four modalities documented in Venezuela, Colombia, Peru, Chile, and the United States. Each modality exploits a specific vulnerability of the target population.

■ 1. Fraudulent Employment Offer (Enganche)

The most frequent and most extensively documented method. Recruiters — known as "enganchadores" — post announcements on social media (Instagram, Facebook, TikTok, WhatsApp) offering employment as waitresses, dancers, domestic workers, or promoters in countries including Colombia, Peru, Chile, Panama, and the United

States, with apparently attractive salaries in dollars. Offers include paid travel and accommodation. Profiles are designed to appear legitimate, with photographs of real workplaces and references from supposedly satisfied former employees. When the victim arrives at her destination, she discovers the offered job does not exist and that she has incurred a "debt" for transport and accommodation that can only be repaid through sexual exploitation. HSToday has documented that TdA recruiters also operate pornographic websites and arrange sexual services through WhatsApp and Snapchat, targeting victims through social media with fake job postings.

■ **2. The Loverboy — The Romantic Deception**
A Tren de Aragua member establishes a romantic relationship with a young woman in Venezuela but also in transit countries. The U.S. Department of State and HSToday have extensively documented this pattern: the recruiter romantically "captures" the victim, builds trust over weeks or months, then proposes they migrate together toward a country with better opportunities. Once at the destination, the relationship is revealed as a trap: the victim is "handed over" to TdA's criminal structure and converted into a "multada." This method is particularly insidious because the victim's emotional bond with the trafficker makes her less likely to self-identify as a victim and more likely to protect her trafficker in subsequent investigations.

■ **3. Progressive Indebtedness — The Pagadiario**

Particularly documented in Colombia, this method exploits the extreme economic vulnerability of Venezuelan migrants. The U.S. Department of State's 2025 Trafficking in Persons (TIP) Report documents how TdA "gained the trust of their victims by housing them in pagadiarios — daily-rate lodgings — in Colombia, providing them food, allowing them to incur daily debts, and, when they are unable to pay, exploiting them in sex trafficking." The debt becomes the control mechanism. It can never be fully settled because recruiters inflate figures and add "interest," fines, and arbitrary charges. The State Department also confirms TdA "allegedly marked women and girls behind their ears to prove ownership" — a physical ownership marking that constitutes a high-specificity victim identification indicator.

■ 4. Direct Coercion and Kidnapping

In areas with the greatest territorial control — especially border zones and migration routes — recruitment can be directly coercive: women and young people are intercepted at crossing points, threatened with violence against themselves or their companions, and forced to "join" the organization. In Venezuela, Biesney José Ocanto López, identified as TdA-linked, was arrested in Aragua while attempting to transport a minor he had deceived through a fake online profile with job offers, with plans to take her through Colombia to Peru for sexual exploitation.

Phase 2: Transit — The Routes of Crime

Once recruited, the victim is transported through a network of transnational routes that the Tren de Aragua controls wholly or partially. Knowledge of these routes — their entry points, transit nodes, transport modalities, and control mechanisms — is operational intelligence directly applicable to border security and investigative agencies.

Route	Documented trajectory	Control methods	U.S. destination
Route 1: Andean	Venezuela (Táchira) → Colombia (Cúcuta/La Parada) → Ecuador → Peru (Lima) → Chile (Santiago/Tarapacá)	*Travel debt, document retention, armed escorts at crossing points*	Can continue to Mexico and U.S. via Central America
Route 2: Darién	Venezuela/Colombia → Darién Gap → Panama → Costa Rica/Nicaragua → Mexico → U.S.	*"Protection" debt in Darién, sexual violence in transit, terror control*	Texas, Florida, New York (primary documented destinations)
Route 3: Caribbean	Venezuela (coasts) → Trinidad & Tobago/Aruba/Curaçao → Dominican Republic → Puerto Rico/U.S.	*Smuggling vessels, agents on each transit island*	Florida, New York (primary entry via island territory)
Route 4: Brazilian	Venezuela (Roraima/Bolívar) → Brazil (Manaus/São Paulo) → Argentina → possible onward transit	*Alliance with Brazil's Primeiro Comando da Capital (PCC)*	Lower documented volume direct to U.S.; more frequent

			settlement point
Route 5: Lateral	Venezuela → Colombia (La Parada) → Ecuador → Mexico → U.S. border crossing	*"All-inclusive travel packages" devolving into bondage; coordination with Mexican cartels on Mexico-U.S. segment*	Texas (El Paso, McAllen), California

Within the transit journey, regardless of the route used, the organization applies a consistent set of transit control techniques documented across multiple jurisdictions:

- **Document Confiscation (18 U.S.C. § 1592)**

  Passports and identity documents are confiscated at the moment of "recruitment" or at the journey's start. Without documents, the victim is unable to contact authorities, request consular help, or prove her identity. Document retention is a federal offense under 18 U.S.C. § 1592 and a near-universal element of documented TdA trafficking schemes. Evidence of confiscated documents in a stash house or on a suspect's person constitutes direct evidence of trafficking conduct.

- **Physical Ownership Marking**

The U.S. Department of State's 2025 TIP Report on Colombia documents that TdA "allegedly marked women and girls behind their ears to prove ownership." This physical marking — which may take the form of tattoos, scars, or burns — is a high-relevance victim identification indicator for medical personnel, nurses, social workers, and agents conducting victim assessments. Its presence, combined with other indicators, constitutes powerful evidence of trafficking victimization.

- **The Controlled Coyote**

  Transport during transit is handled by facilitators — "coyotes" — who are themselves either band members or contractors operating under its direction. The coyote is responsible for the victim during his segment of the journey and "delivers" her to the next network node. This transport segmentation complicates investigation because an arrested coyote may know only his segment of the route, not the complete network. Developing cooperating coyotes with route-segment knowledge is one of the most effective investigative techniques for mapping the full TdA trafficking infrastructure.

- **Preventive Terror**

  Before the journey begins, victims are told — often with fabricated or real evidence — of the consequences of attempting to escape or report: accounts of other women killed, violence videos, and explicit threats against family members in Venezuela whose address the organization has already documented. The U.S. Department of the Treasury confirms that "when victims seek to escape this exploitation, Tren de Aragua members often kill them and publicize their deaths as a threat to others." This preventive terror mechanism dramatically reduces escape attempts and creates fear-based compliance that makes constant physical control unnecessary.

Phase 3: Destination — Control at the Exploitation Site

Upon arriving at their destination — whether a Latin American city, a Venezuelan diaspora community in the United States, or any other point in the network — the victim is integrated into TdA's exploitation operation. The control mechanism at the exploitation site combines physical, psychological, financial, and relational instruments.

■ **The Stash House**

Victims are housed in "stash houses" — apartments or houses controlled by the band where multiple victims live under the supervision of a controller. The April 2025 Southern District of New York indictment describes how TdA and its splinter faction Anti-Tren "find real estate to use as stash houses where victims are held" and are "transported across the country using weapons and intimidation." ICE documented this pattern in the Nashville, Tennessee operation, where eight TdA-linked individuals operated a commercial sex and sex trafficking enterprise from city motels from July 2022 through March 2024.

■ **The Digital Exploitation Platform**

TdA does not limit sexual exploitation to the traditional in-person prostitution model. It has developed a diversified digital platform including: non-consensual pornography websites; advertising of "escort services" through WhatsApp, Snapchat, and Telegram; band-controlled camgirl platforms; and distribution networks for documented sexual abuse content. This digital diversification increases revenue, geographically disperses criminal activity, and makes victim identification more difficult, as victims can be exploited from an apartment without physical mobilization.

■ **The Unpayable Debt as Permanent Bondage**

The most effective financial control mechanism is the "debt" the victim supposedly owes for her transport, accommodation, food, and "protection." This debt is deliberately constructed to be mathematically impossible to settle: daily interest is added, "fines" are charged for any rule infractions, and any earnings are partially deducted from the debt while the rest is retained as organizational "profit." ICE and DOJ have documented schemes where an original debt of $500 grows to $10,000 or more within weeks through this mechanism. Debt bondage as a control instrument is an explicit federal offense under 18 U.S.C. § 1584 and constitutes the "means" element of the trafficking offense under 18 U.S.C. § 1591.

Phase 4: Retention — How the Organization Keeps Its Victims

Victim retention in the exploitation system is not maintained solely through direct coercion. TdA employs a sophisticated set of retention mechanisms that exploit the psychological, relational, and migratory vulnerabilities of its victims.

- **Fear of Immigration Authorities**

  Victims in irregular immigration status in the United States are threatened with being reported to immigration authorities if they attempt to escape or report. This threat is particularly effective in the post-2025 environment, where increased deportation pressure has heightened the perceived vulnerability of undocumented immigrants. The organization deliberately exploits deportation fear as a retention instrument. This is why agents must communicate explicitly, at the outset of any encounter with a potential victim, that she will not be prosecuted or deported for reporting her situation, and that she may qualify for a T visa.

- **Threats Against Family Members in Venezuela**

  The organization systematically documents the identity and location of its victims' family members in Venezuela. Threats against those family members — credible and executable given TdA's confirmed operational reach in Venezuela — are the most powerful retention instrument available to the band. A victim who would attempt escape if only her own safety were at risk can be retained indefinitely by the threat against her children, parents, or siblings in Venezuela. This cross-border coercive capacity is one of the most distinctive and dangerous features of TdA's trafficking model.

- **Psychological Manipulation and Trauma Bonding**

  Trafficking researchers have documented that TdA recruiters use psychological manipulation techniques consistent with "trauma bonding" — the emotional bond that can develop between a victim and her exploiter as a survival mechanism. This is especially frequent in cases initiated through the "loverboy" method, where the victim has built a genuine emotional bond with the recruiter before being exploited. The practical consequence for investigators is that victims may not self-identify as such, may actively protect their exploiters, and may recant statements in judicial proceedings. Understanding trauma bonding is not a defense for perpetrators — it is essential context for investigators and prosecutors building victim-centered cases.

III. Specific Routes to the United States

3.1 The Darién Gap: The Jungle as Trafficking Corridor

No point in the journey to the United States has concentrated more violence, exploitation, and human suffering than the Darién Gap — the impenetrable jungle connecting Colombia and Panama, whose crossing requires four to seven days of walking under extreme conditions. In 2023, over 520,000 migrants crossed the Darién, an unprecedented number in the route's history. The Tren de Aragua was present at every segment of that corridor, with research from the Secure Free Society Initiative and the International Organization for Migration confirming TdA as a primary perpetrator of sexual violence against women and girls in transit.

In the Darién, TdA operates through "protection packages": migrants — including trafficking victims who don't know they are — pay between $300 and $2,000 for "protection" during the crossing. For those who cannot pay, the debt becomes the first link in the bondage chain. For women and young people in the group, "protection" frequently includes demands for sexual services from the band's "guides." After the Darién, the route continues through Panama, Costa Rica, Nicaragua, Honduras, Guatemala, and finally Mexico. In each of these countries, TdA maintains operational nodes: controllers who supervise victim transit, coordinators managing payments between route segments, and "delivery" agents who transfer victim custody to the next chain link.

DHS has confirmed to media that TdA has a presence in at least 46 U.S. states. The organization has established agreements with Mexican cartels — including the Sinaloa Cartel, according to DHS investigators — to manage the final crossing into the United States, particularly in Texas and California. This cross-cartel cooperation has been documented in both the Maduro indictment and separate DEA intelligence assessments.

3.2 The Nashville Case: Documented U.S. Operations

> *"We were told we were going to work at a restaurant. That we would earn well. That the owner was Venezuelan like us. When we arrived at the motel, they took our phones and told us how much we owed. There was no restaurant. Only the motel and the rooms."*

— Victim testimony from the Nashville, Tennessee operation, 2024-2025 (identity protected)

The Nashville, Tennessee case, dismantled by ICE and the Tennessee Bureau of Investigation in February 2025, is one of the most publicly documented cases of TdA operations on American soil. For nearly two years — from July 2022 through March 2024 — a network of eight individuals with documented TdA ties operated a commercial sex and sex trafficking enterprise from Nashville motels.

The defendants — including family members Yilibeth del Carmen Rivero-De Caldera and her son Kleiver Daniel Mota-Rivero — face sex trafficking conspiracy charges under 18 U.S.C. § 1591, with a maximum penalty of life imprisonment, for "conspiring to use force, fraud, and coercion to compel women into commercial sex acts for the defendants' profit." The indictment explicitly describes use of "alleged ties to TdA and its reputation for violence" as a coercion instrument against victims — the threat of gang membership was itself the terror instrument.

3.3 New York: The Epicenter of TdA Trafficking on American Soil

The Southern District of New York has been the federal district most actively prosecuting TdA trafficking cases. In April 2025, 27 members or associates of the Tren de Aragua and its splinter faction "Anti-Tren" were charged in two superseding indictments for racketeering conspiracy, sex trafficking conspiracy, drug trafficking conspiracy, robbery, and firearms offenses.

U.S. Attorney Jay Clayton described the crimes in unambiguous terms: "Tren de Aragua is in the business of murder, sex trafficking and intimidation, and they brought that business to New York while being unlawfully present in the United States." The defendants "exerted ruthless control over sex trafficking victims through intimidation, brutality, and threats of violence against them and their loved ones — leaving lasting trauma in their wake." The indictment documents two victim murders in the Bronx, multiple attempted murders of fleeing victims in New York and Florida, home invasion robberies, and a sophisticated multi-state operation with presence confirmed in New Jersey, Illinois, and Washington.

IV. The Federal Legal Framework: Tools for Prosecution

Human trafficking perpetrated by the Tren de Aragua activates multiple federal statutes that provide a robust legal arsenal for prosecution. Knowledge of these statutes is essential for prosecutors and investigators developing the strongest case theories and obtaining convictions commensurate with the gravity of the conduct.

- **18 U.S.C. § 1591 — Sex Trafficking of Children and Adults**

  The primary statute for sex trafficking prosecution. Criminalizes the recruitment, harboring, transportation, provision, obtaining, or maintaining of a person for commercial sex through force, fraud, or coercion (or when the victim is under 18, regardless of means). Maximum penalty: life imprisonment when the victim is under 14 years of age or when force is used. Mandatory minimum of 15 years for victims under 14. This is the primary charge in most documented U.S. TdA trafficking cases.

- **18 U.S.C. § 1590 — Trafficking for Involuntary Servitude**

Criminalizes the recruitment, harboring, transportation, or provision of persons for forced labor. Relevant for TdA labor trafficking victims — including illegal mining workers and domestic workers in conditions of servitude. Maximum penalty: 20 years imprisonment.

■ 18 U.S.C. § 1592 — Document Confiscation

Criminalizes the seizure or destruction of trafficking victims' identification documents. Document retention is near-universal in documented TdA schemes. This charge is frequently stacked with sex trafficking charges to expand defendants' criminal exposure.

■ 18 U.S.C. § 1584 — Involuntary Debt Servitude

Directly applicable to the "multadas" scheme and the "travel debt" mechanism. Criminalizes maintaining persons in servitude through coercion including threat of adverse legal or financial consequences. The unpayable debt structure described in this chapter falls squarely within this statute's elements.

■ 18 U.S.C. §§ 1961-1968 (RICO) with Trafficking as Predicate

Trafficking is a predicate offense under RICO, enabling prosecution of the entire TdA criminal enterprise — not just direct perpetrators — when trafficking forms part of the pattern of racketeering activity. RICO charges carry up to 20 years per predicate act, plus criminal forfeiture of enterprise assets. The December 2025 SDNY indictment of Nino Guerrero uses precisely this theory, linking trafficking within the broader racketeering enterprise.

- **■ 22 U.S.C. § 7101 et seq. — The Trafficking Victims Protection Act (TVPA)**

  Beyond defining offenses, the TVPA establishes fundamental victim rights: right to support services, to a T visa (permitting U.S. stay during investigation and prosecution), and to not be prosecuted for offenses committed because of trafficking. Correct TVPA application — including early victim identification and benefits offering — is not merely a legal mandate but an investigative tool: victims who receive protection and support are significantly more likely to cooperate as witnesses.

🔍 THE T VISA: THE MOST UNDERUTILIZED TOOL IN TdA CASES

The T visa allows trafficking victims to remain in the United States for up to four years if they cooperate with authorities in investigation and prosecution. It is an extraordinarily valuable investigative instrument: it converts victims who would otherwise be terrified of deportation into protected witnesses with immigration status. However, DHS studies show the T visa is chronically underutilized in Venezuelan community trafficking cases, partly because field agents don't always correctly identify victims or inform them of their rights. Every agent working TdA cases should be fully familiar with T visa application procedures and victim identification criteria under TVPA. Failure to advise potential victims of T visa availability can constitute a due process issue in subsequent prosecutorial proceedings.

V. Key Federal Cases: What the Formal Indictments Say

- **CASE 1: Southern District of New York — Nino Guerrero RICO Indictment (December 2025)**

  The racketeering indictment against Héctor Rusthenford Guerrero Flores in the SDNY explicitly includes human trafficking as part of the racketeering pattern. It documents how Venezuelan women were "smuggled from Venezuela into countries including Colombia, Peru, and the United States and forced into commercial sex work to repay debts." The indictment spans acts from 2005 through 2025, establishing scheme continuity across two decades and positioning the trafficking operation as a core element of the criminal enterprise.

- **CASE 2: Middle District of Tennessee — Nashville (February 2025)**

  Eight defendants with documented TdA ties charged with sex trafficking conspiracy under 18 U.S.C. § 1591. Operation ran July 2022 through March 2024 in Nashville motels. Defendants explicitly used "TdA's reputation for violence" as a coercion tool. Maximum penalty for the conspiracy: life imprisonment. This case illustrates TdA's ability to establish trafficking operations in mid-size American cities far from traditional criminal hubs.

- **CASE 3: Southern District of New York — TdA and Anti-Tren (April 2025)**

  27 members or associates charged with racketeering, sex trafficking conspiracy, drug trafficking, robbery, and firearms offenses. U.S. Attorney Clayton: defendants

"exerted ruthless control over sex trafficking victims through intimidation, brutality, and threats of violence against them and their loved ones." Documented crimes include two victim murders in the Bronx and multiple attempted murders of fleeing victims. Operations confirmed in New York, New Jersey, Illinois, and Washington.

- **CASE 4: District of Colorado — Aurora (2024-2025)**

    The nationally prominent Aurora case included explicit human trafficking and kidnapping charges as part of the TdA RICO operation in Colorado. Apartment complexes used as operational bases functioned partially as stash houses for trafficking victims. The case also documented TdA's use of armed presence in residential buildings as a territorial control and victim detention mechanism.

- **CASE 5: Peru — U.S.-Peru Joint Operation (January 2025)**

    A joint operation between Peru's National Police and U.S. agencies freed more than 80 TdA trafficking victims in Lima. Researchers documented that "within days, replacement cells reemerged" — illustrating the franchise model's resilience against dismantling operations and the need for sustained, multi-jurisdiction pressure rather than isolated interdiction actions.

VI. The Victims: Who They Are and How to Help Them

6.1 Victim Identification Indicators

The following behavioral, physical, and situational indicators — when present in combination, not in isolation — constitute the evidence-based standard for identifying potential TdA trafficking victims. No single indicator is conclusive; their convergence, assessed holistically, is what justifies a trafficking determination.

- **Behavioral indicators**

  Appears disoriented, fearful, or submissive; defers all questions to an accompanying person who is not identified as a known family member; avoids eye contact with officials; gives inconsistent or scripted answers about her work or accommodation situation; does not know the address of where she is living or the name of her employer; shows signs of physical abuse; does not control her own identification documents or money.

- **Physical indicators**

  Markings behind the ears or other unusual markings inconsistent with decorative tattoos; signs of recent physical trauma; evidence of malnutrition or medical neglect; wearing inappropriate clothing for weather (often caused by being moved from one climate to another without adequate resources); presence of multiple women of similar age and apparent ethnicity in the same location with limited freedom of movement.

- **Situational indicators**

Accommodation paid by a third party not present or not identified; motel residence with a high turnover of Venezuelan women; multiple women present at one address who claim not to know each other; presence of sexually explicit materials or evidence of commercial sex activity; large amounts of cash or prepaid cards controlled by a third party; and knowledge of the TdA lexicon — particularly the word "multada" regarding her own situation.

6.2 Why Victims Do Not Self-Identify: Barriers to Reporting

One of the most critical characteristics for professionals interacting with potential TdA victims is understanding why victims frequently do not self-identify, do not report, and sometimes actively protect their exploiters. These barriers are not irrational choices: they are predictable and understandable psychological responses to the violence and control in which these individuals are trapped.

■ **Fear of deportation**

The threat of being reported to ICE and deported is the most effective silencing instrument available to exploiters. An agent or officer who encounters a potential victim must communicate explicitly, at the outset of any interaction, that the victim will not be prosecuted or deported for disclosing her situation, and that she may qualify for T visa protection.

- **Fear of reprisals against family in Venezuela**

  Threats against family members remaining in Venezuela are credible and executable given TdA's operational reach. Without protection extended to those family members, reporting is perceived as an unacceptable risk. Connecting victims with organizations that have experience in cross-border family protection is an essential component of victim-centered investigation.

- **Active disinformation by exploiters**

  Victims are frequently told — falsely — that sex trafficking is not a crime in the U.S., or that American justice will prosecute them as criminals. Exploiters also spread disinformation that authorities are corrupt or allied with the band, discouraging any reporting attempt.

- **Trauma bonding and dissociation**

  Victims subjected to intense, prolonged trauma frequently develop adaptive psychological responses that can appear, from outside, as voluntary cooperation or loyalty to exploiters. Trauma bonding, dissociation, and post-traumatic stress disorder are documented, understandable responses that justice professionals must understand before evaluating a victim's credibility or behavior. Under TVPA, victim credibility is assessed with explicit recognition that trafficking victims may exhibit behavior that appears inconsistent with victimhood because of these psychological mechanisms.

🔍 RECOMMENDED VICTIM INTERVIEW PROTOCOL

When interviewing a potential TdA trafficking victim: (1) Separate the person from any unidentified companion before beginning — never interview a potential victim in the presence of her suspected trafficker. (2) Explicitly inform her, at the outset, of non-prosecution protection under TVPA and T visa availability. (3) Use a qualified interpreter in Venezuelan Spanish — dialect and argot matter for building trust. (4) Conduct the interview in a physically safe space, away from the exploitation environment. (5) Do not pressure for statements about perpetrators in the first interview: prioritize assessment of immediate safety, health, and housing needs. (6) Involve specialized trafficking victim support organizations for post-interview accompaniment. (7) Document all physical indicators observed during the interview, including markings, signs of trauma, and document retention evidence.

VII. Chapter Summary: What This Chapter Demands of Professionals

Human trafficking perpetrated by the Tren de Aragua is, in all its dimensions, a crime of systematic brutality and operational sophistication that demands equally sophisticated responses from the justice system and society.

■ **For field agents and investigators**

Trafficking victim identification requires specific training in documented TdA indicators. The term "multada," document retention, unpayable debts, physical ownership marking, and threats against Venezuelan family members are high-specificity indicators. The T visa is an investigative tool that must be actively offered. Stash houses, low-cost motels with a high turnover of Venezuelan women, and "escort" advertising networks on apps are the most frequent operational environments.

■ **For federal prosecutors**

The combination of RICO (18 U.S.C. §§ 1961-1968) with trafficking statutes as predicate offenses allows building indictments that reflect the true scale and entrepreneurial nature of TdA's criminal activity. Racketeering prosecution linking trafficking with extortion, contract killing, and money laundering within the same criminal enterprise generates higher, more appropriate penalties than isolated prosecutions.

■ **For immigration judges and attorneys**

TdA trafficking victims frequently enter the immigration system without self-identifying. Immigration judges and attorneys must be equipped to recognize the indicators described in this chapter and ensure victims are correctly identified before any immigration determination is made that could result in their deportation.

■ **For legislators and policymakers**

Combating TdA trafficking requires sustained funding for: (a) first-responder training in victim identification; (b) specialized shelters for Venezuelan trafficking victims; (c) culturally competent psychotrauma support services; (d) international cooperation to protect victims' family members in Venezuela; and (e) the Venezuelan Criminal Records Verification Program detailed in Chapter Ten, which would enable access to critical information currently blocked by Venezuela's state collapse.

■ **For the public**

TdA trafficking occurs in roadside motels, in apartments in ordinary neighborhoods, in Instagram and WhatsApp ads, in the same buildings where we live and work. Recognizing the indicators — women with restricted freedom of movement, documents held by third parties, no control over their own income, visible fear in the presence of their companion — and reporting them to the National Human Trafficking Hotline (1-888-373-7888) or 911 can save a life.

— END OF CHAPTER FOUR —

National Human Trafficking Hotline: 1-888-373-7888 | Text: "HELP" or "INFO" to 233733

CHAPTER FIVE

The Tren de Aragua in the United States

Documented presence, calibrated threat assessment, and the Venezuelan intelligence gap

Introductory Note

This chapter bridges the criminological analysis of previous chapters with the concrete operational reality facing security officials, legislators, and citizens in the United States. Here, the Tren de Aragua ceases to be a phenomenon "out there" and becomes a documented, active, and expanding threat within American territory.

The debate about the actual magnitude of that presence has frequently been more political than analytical. This chapter applies the correct methodological standard: distinguishing between what the evidence shows, what the evidence suggests, and what is political projection without solid factual basis.

I. The Documented Presence: What We Know with Certainty

1.1 Federal prosecution statistics

The most reliable data on Tren de Aragua presence in the United States comes from the federal criminal prosecution system. From January 20, 2025, when the Trump administration designated TdA as a Foreign Terrorist Organization, through December 2025, the Department of Justice filed federal charges against over 260 band members in five districts: Colorado, Nebraska, New Mexico, the Southern District of New York, and the Southern District of Texas.

The Department of Homeland Security (DHS) confirmed to several media outlets that TdA has a reported presence in at least 46 states. Of approximately 7,000 gang member arrests conducted by ICE since early 2025, 1,232 have confirmed TdA ties — making it the Venezuelan criminal organization with the largest identified presence on American soil.

In December 2025, DOJ announced the unsealing of indictments against over 70 additional TdA-linked individuals across five districts, including RICO conspiracy, murder, extortion, kidnapping, money laundering, and controlled substance trafficking charges. The Joint Task Force Vulcan, expanded specifically to address TdA, coordinates the FBI, DEA, HSI, ATF, U.S.

Marshals, and Bureau of Prisons across 13 U.S. Attorney's Offices nationwide.

1.2 Documented geographic presence in the U.S.

Cities with solid documentation of TdA operations on American soil — based on federal indictments, confirmed detentions, and security agency reports — include the following priority jurisdictions:

- **New York City (The Bronx and Queens)**

  The jurisdiction with the largest number of federally prosecuted TdA members in 2025. The April 2025 SDNY indictment describes sex trafficking operations, victim murders in the Bronx, armed robberies in Yonkers, and a network structure reaching New Jersey, Illinois, and Washington. The city has approximately 150,000 Venezuelan residents, the largest concentration in the U.S. Northeast.

- **Aurora / Denver, Colorado**

  The 2024-2025 Aurora case generated the most national attention. Documented TdA operations include control of apartment complexes, human trafficking, drug distribution, and a RICO conspiracy indictment spanning May 2024 through March 2025. Aurora's experience has become the reference case for understanding TdA's neighborhood-level territorial control methodology in American communities.

- **Houston and Dallas, Texas**

Texas was the first state to designate TdA as a terrorist organization, in September 2024, after documented increases in extortion and retail theft rings in San Antonio and Houston. The Southern District of Texas has prosecuted multiple TdA cases, and Rio Grande crossing points are documented entry points for the band's human trafficking operations.

- **Miami, Florida**

  Miami is home to the largest Venezuelan community in the United States, estimated at over 200,000 people. TdA has established extortion operations targeting this community, and Florida was cited in the April 2025 SDNY indictment as a jurisdiction where murder conspiracies targeting trafficking victims were executed.

- **Nashville, Tennessee and other mid-size cities**

  The Nashville operation documented in this book demonstrates that TdA does not limit its presence to major metropolises. The band follows Venezuelan communities regardless of city size, establishing operations in any market with sufficient diaspora concentration and exploitable local institutional weakness.

II. The Nino Guerrero Indictment: The Definitive Charge (December 2025)

On December 18, 2025, the Department of Justice unsealed a RICO racketeering indictment against Héctor

Rusthenford Guerrero Flores in the Southern District of New York. This indictment represents the most complete and definitive publicly available legal document on the Tren de Aragua as a criminal enterprise. Its most important elements for security professionals are:

- **Temporal scope: 2005-2025**

  The indictment documents 20 years of continuous criminal activity, establishing the "continuity" required by RICO and positioning TdA as a criminal enterprise with long-term institutional history, not an emerging gang. This temporal scope has direct implications for the RICO "enterprise" evidentiary standard and for forfeiture of assets accumulated over two decades.

- **Geographic scope: multiple countries and multiple U.S. states**

  The indictment documents operations in Venezuela, Colombia, Peru, Chile, Brazil, Mexico, Spain, and multiple U.S. states including New York, Colorado, New Mexico, Texas, Nebraska, Illinois, and Florida. This geographic scope activates federal extraterritorial jurisdiction under RICO and under mutual legal help treaties (MLATs) with countries where the band operates.

- **Drug trafficking and cocaine escort charges**

  The indictment charges Guerrero Flores with "directing and supporting escort services for cocaine shipments and controlling coastal storage facilities" in coordination with Venezuela's Cartel de los Soles. This is consistent with the

January 3, 2026 indictment against Maduro, in which Guerrero Flores is a co-defendant in the same scheme.

- **Trafficking as a racketeering element**

  Human trafficking is an explicit predicate offense in the Guerrero Flores RICO indictment, directly connecting the "multadas" scheme to the organization's supreme leadership and eliminating any argument that trafficking is a peripheral activity performed by low-level operators without connection to the pran.

III. The Analytical Debate: A Calibrated Threat Assessment

American policy on the Tren de Aragua in 2025 developed in intense political pressure that, in several instances, led to claims about the band that exceeded what available evidence supported. A calibrated assessment — the foundation of effective security policy — requires distinguishing between three levels of certainty:

- **High certainty — what evidence shows indisputably**

  TdA has documented operational presence in multiple American cities. It has committed murders, extortion, human trafficking, and drug distribution on American soil. Its members have been prosecuted in five federal districts with convictions or pending indictments. The FTO designation is legally sustained.

■ **Medium certainty — what evidence suggests but does not conclusively show**

The full extent of TdA presence across the 46 states where DHS reports activity varies enormously in density and organization. The distinction between genuinely organized TdA cells and criminal activity by Venezuelan individuals using the band's name without real affiliation is an analytical gap agencies are still resolving. The direct connection with the Venezuelan government as operational direction is supported by the DOJ indictment but questioned by the National Intelligence Council assessment.

■ **Low certainty — what is political exaggeration without solid factual basis**

The description of TdA as an "invasion" of American territory under the Alien Enemies Act was rejected by a federal appellate court on September 2, 2025. The claim that virtually all Venezuelans deported in March 2025 where TdA members was contradicted by multiple journalistic investigations and by the El Salvador government itself in cases of demonstrably innocent deportees.

🔍 **SECURITY POLICY IMPLICATION**

Effective security policy against TdA requires analytical precision. Threat overestimation leads to collective criminalization of the Venezuelan community — which is in its vast majority victim, not perpetrator — destroying the community trust essential for witness cooperation. Underestimation leads to insufficient resources and inadequate strategies. The balance point is evidence-based assessment.

IV. The Information Gap: The Venezuelan Records Problem

The most significant operational challenge for American security agencies working Tren de Aragua cases is not identifying suspects on American soil — it is verifying their criminal backgrounds in Venezuela. Without access to Venezuelan penitentiary system records, Public Ministry databases, or Venezuelan state criminal intelligence records, immigration agents, federal prosecutors, and immigration judges decide about individuals whose criminal history in their country of origin is, practically speaking, invisible.

This information gap is not accidental: it was a deliberate consequence of Venezuela's institutional collapse under Maduro, which made international judicial cooperation with Venezuela practically impossible. The January 3, 2026 indictment against Maduro explicitly identified the Venezuelan state's refusal to cooperate with international intelligence agencies as an element of the criminal scheme: origin-country impunity was part of the business model.

With the Maduro government dismantled and a transitional administration in Venezuela, there is for the first time in two decades a genuine possibility of establishing cooperation mechanisms for access to those records. The Venezuelan Criminal Records Verification Program — detailed in Chapter Ten — is specifically designed to capitalize on this historic window of opportunity, leveraging the deep institutional knowledge of the Venezuelan system that no American agency possesses on its own.

V. Summary: The Threat Landscape in 2026

The Tren de Aragua in 2026 is an organization in transition: it has lost its Venezuelan operational base (Tocorón) and its primary state protector (the Maduro regime), but has built abroad a decentralized, resilient criminal infrastructure that continues operating with increasing autonomy. For the United States, this means:

- **The threat does not disappear with Maduro**
  The cells established in the 46 reported American jurisdictions will continue operating independently of

political developments in Venezuela. The absence of the Venezuelan state umbrella may even accelerate the operational autonomy of those cells.

- **The intelligence opportunity must be seized urgently**

  The Venezuelan transition opens an unprecedented window to records and intelligence. This window can close. Agencies must act now to establish the necessary cooperation channels, with the correct institutional mediators.

- **The TdA-migrant distinction is an operational and ethical imperative**

  Effective security policy against TdA depends on the trust of Venezuelan communities, who are the band's primary victims and the most valuable witnesses available. That trust is destroyed when security policy collectively criminalizes the community. Precise distinction is, paradoxically, both the correct ethical position and the most operationally efficient strategy.

— END OF CHAPTER FIVE —

CHAPTER SIX

The Financial Architecture of Crime

Revenue sources, money laundering, and TdA financial prosecution tools

Introductory Note: Why Money Matters

Criminal organizations are, at their core, economic enterprises. The Tren de Aragua is no exception. Its crimes — extortion, trafficking, contract killing, gota a gota, drug trafficking — are income-generation mechanisms. What distinguishes a sophisticated criminal organization from a street gang is its capacity to convert those illicit proceeds into legitimate, lasting wealth that is invisible to authorities. That conversion — money laundering — is the function that closes the criminal cycle and allows the organization to survive and grow.

For prosecutors, financial analysts, judges, and financial regulators working TdA cases, understanding the band's financial model is as important as understanding its criminal model. Following the money is not just a catchphrase: it is the most effective investigative strategy available for dismantling complex criminal organizations.

I. The TdA Economy: Revenue Sources and Scale

1.1 The revenue generation portfolio

The Tren de Aragua operates an extraordinarily diversified income generation portfolio. This diversification is not accidental: it is a deliberate strategy that maximizes total revenue, distributes legal detection risk across multiple offense typifications, and allows the organization to adapt to changes in the law enforcement environment without losing income-generation capacity.

- **Extortion (vacuna): $3.5M-$10M annually estimated (Tocorón + proximate communities only)**

  The internal "causa" generated $3.5M annually just from Tocorón inmates, per Venezuelan authorities' estimates. The vacuna applied to businesses and residents in band-controlled communities generates additional figures that Heritage Foundation and Secure Free Society Institute researchers estimate at multiple additional millions in Venezuela and operating countries.

- **Sexual exploitation and trafficking: $500-$2,000 per victim monthly (multiplied by dozens or hundreds of active victims)**

  The "multadas" scheme generates recurring revenue per victim. If the active victim network at any given time is 200 people — a conservative estimate given the organization's documented reach — monthly revenue from this source reaches between $100,000 and $400,000. Digital sexual exploitation platforms multiply these numbers by eliminating the logistical costs of in-person sex work.

■ Illegal gold mining: $1.7M daily according to documented sources

TdA controls illegal gold mines in Venezuela, extracting between 30 and 50 kilograms daily, equivalent to approximately $1.7 million at 2025 market prices. This is potentially the largest individual revenue component for the organization in Venezuela. Control of illegal mining also gives the band access to a physical asset — gold — that is easier to launder than cash because it can be melted and sold as legal precious metal.

■ Gota a gota: 20-100% monthly rates on loans to immigrant communities

The gota a gota model is extraordinarily profitable: a loan portfolio of $100,000 at 50% monthly generates $50,000 monthly in interest income alone, independent of principal. That the debt is mathematically unpayable means the "portfolio" becomes a permanent income source.

■ Criminal services: contract killing, logistics, escort

As described in Chapter Three, TdA offers criminal services to other organizations: contract killings priced at $3,000-$50,000, trafficking logistics, drug shipment escort, and border point control. The Nino Guerrero indictment explicitly documents "escort services for cocaine shipments" as an organizational revenue source.

II. Money Laundering: Converting Crime into Wealth

2.1 The three classic stages and how TdA applies them

Money laundering follows, in its fundamental structure, three stages that criminological and financial literature has extensively documented: placement, layering, and integration. The Tren de Aragua applies these stages with variations adapted to its specific operational context.

■ Stage 1: Placement — Introducing cash into the financial system

Cash generated by TdA's criminal operations — especially extortion, trafficking, and gota a gota — must be introduced into the financial system somehow. Documented techniques include: structuring (multiple small deposits avoiding $10,000 reporting thresholds under the Bank Secrecy Act); use of cash-intensive businesses (laundromats, restaurants, grocery stores, beauty salons in Venezuelan communities) as placement points; and international transfers through informal money transmitters (exchange houses) operating outside American regulatory frameworks.

■ Stage 2: Layering — Obscuring the origin

Once in the financial system, funds are moved through multiple transaction layers designed to obscure the trail to their criminal origin. TdA uses: international transfers to multiple jurisdictions (especially to Venezuela, Colombia, Peru, and Spain, where the organization has presence); rapid buy-and-sell of real estate in high-liquidity markets; use of third-party accounts (individuals without criminal records who lend their identity for payment); and cryptocurrencies, especially for cross-jurisdiction transactions where speed and pseudonymity complicate detection.

■ Stage 3: Integration — The "clean" money returns to the legal circuit

In the final stage, laundered funds are reinvested in legitimate assets or additional criminal operations. The most frequent integration assets include: food and service businesses in Venezuelan communities (restaurants, barbershops, transportation services); real estate in countries with high Venezuelan diaspora concentration; and luxury vehicles that can be sold or transferred without triggering the same reporting thresholds as bank transfers.

2.2 Emerging financial crimes: jackpotting and ATM theft

The DOJ revealed in December 2025 that TdA "has developed an additional source of revenue through financial crimes that target financial institutions throughout the United States, including using jackpotting to steal millions of dollars in cash." Jackpotting is a sophisticated cybercrime technique that uses malicious hardware or software to cause ATMs to dispense cash without authorization. Eighty-seven TdA members were indicted in Nebraska for nationwide bank and ATM theft conducted to fund their criminal operations.

The incorporation of sophisticated financial crimes into TdA's criminal portfolio represents a significant organizational evolution: the band not only commits street-level crimes but has developed capacity in financial and cybercrime — clearly marking its position in the Fourth Wave of organized crime described in Chapter One.

III. Financial Prosecution Tools

The following laws and mechanisms constitute the arsenal for financial prosecution of TdA in the United States:

- **Bank Secrecy Act (31 U.S.C. §§ 5311-5336)**
  Requires financial institutions to report transactions over $10,000 (Currency Transaction Reports) and any suspicious activity that may involve money laundering (Suspicious Activity Reports). Structuring — dividing transactions to avoid these thresholds — is itself a federal offense under 31 U.S.C. § 5324.

- **Money Laundering Control Act (18 U.S.C. §§ 1956-1957)**
  The primary money laundering statute. Criminalizes financial transactions involving proceeds from specifically

unlawful activities. Maximum penalty under § 1956 is 20 years imprisonment and a fine of $500,000 or twice the value of the laundered money. § 1957 specifically criminalizes transactions exceeding $10,000 in criminal proceeds.

- **RICO Forfeiture (18 U.S.C. § 1963)**

  The RICO indictment against TdA activates forfeiture of all criminal enterprise assets: real estate, vehicles, bank accounts, businesses, and any other asset acquired with or derived from racketeering proceeds. RICO forfeiture is one of the most effective instruments for dismantling criminal organizations because it eliminates the capital that funds enterprise continuation.

- **OFAC Sanctions**

  The Department of the Treasury designated TdA as a Significant Transnational Criminal Organization in July 2024 and sanctioned its leadership under the narcotics trafficking sanctions program (SDNTK). In June 2025, OFAC sanctioned Giovanni Vicente Mosquera Serrano, a fugitive TdA leader in Colombia, with the Department of State offering a $3 million reward for information leading to his capture. OFAC sanctions freeze assets under American jurisdiction and prohibit transactions with the designated individuals.

🔍 FINANCIAL RED FLAGS FOR INSTITUTIONS

Financial institutions should train their compliance teams to recognize TdA-specific red flags: (a) multiple small cash deposits to the same account or related accounts, just below the $10,000 threshold (structuring); (b) frequent transfers to Venezuela, Colombia, Peru, or Chile from accounts of individuals without U.S. credit history; (c) laundromat, barbershop, or restaurant businesses in Venezuelan communities with income volumes inconsistent with reported activity; (d) rapid real estate buy-and-sell between related parties; and (e) multiple rent or service payments in cash from the same address to multiple landlords.

IV. Summary: The Follow-the-Money Strategy

The financial prosecution approach is, together with the RICO model, the most effective strategy for dismantling the Tren de Aragua as a criminal enterprise. Unlike individual criminal prosecution — which eliminates individual operators who can be replaced — financial prosecution attacks the capital that funds the operation, the infrastructure that sustains it, and the economic incentives that perpetuate it.

Three operational recommendations emerge from this chapter:

■ **Parallel financial investigations**
Every TdA criminal investigation must have a parallel financial component from its inception. Late incorporation of financial analysis frequently results in loss of assets that

have been transferred or concealed during the criminal investigation period. FBI and IRS-CI financial analysis specialists must be incorporated from day one.

■ **Coordination with FinCEN and financial regulators**

The Financial Crimes Enforcement Network (FinCEN) has access to all Suspicious Activity Reports and Currency Transaction Reports filed by financial institutions. SAR requests on individuals under TdA investigation should be standard practice. FinCEN can also issue Geographic Targeting Orders requiring financial institutions in specific areas to report cash real estate purchases — a tool directly applicable to markets where TdA has documented operations.

■ **International cooperation for offshore assets**

TdA assets in Venezuela, Colombia, Peru, and Chile must be identified and frozen through mutual legal help (MLAT) mechanisms with those countries. The Nino Guerrero and Maduro indictments provide the legal basis for MLAT requests that identify and freeze criminal enterprise assets across multiple jurisdictions simultaneously.

— END OF CHAPTER SIX —

CHAPTER SEVEN

International Legal Framework and Policy Recommendations

Legal tools, legislative agenda, and the role of the Latino Institute for Security Efficiency

Introductory Note: From Analysis to Action

Previous chapters have built a comprehensive picture of the Tren de Aragua: its origin, structure, expansion, crimes, and financing. This chapter finalizes that analysis and converts it into action. For legislators, policymakers, judges, and public security executives, the value of a book like this is measured in the concrete decisions it enables. This chapter is the translation of criminology into policy.

The recommendations that follow emerge from fifteen years of prosecutorial experience in Venezuela, from analysis of the most relevant international legal frameworks, and from systematic study of institutional responses that have demonstrated real effectiveness — and those that have failed. They are not theoretical proposals: they are policy instruments available for immediate implementation.

I. The International Legal Framework: Available Tools

1.1 The Palermo Convention and its protocols

The United Nations Convention against Transnational Organized Crime (Palermo Convention, 2000) and its three protocols — on human trafficking (Palermo Protocol), migrant smuggling, and arms trafficking — constitute the fundamental international legal framework for the transnational prosecution of the Tren de Aragua. The United States, Venezuela (though with historically limited cooperation), and all countries where TdA operates are signatories.

The Palermo Convention mechanisms most directly relevant to TdA cases include: the commitment to criminalize transnational organized crime (Art. 5); extradition mechanisms for identified members found in signatory countries (Art. 16); mutual legal help for obtaining cross-border evidence (Art. 18); forfeiture of organized crime-derived assets (Art. 12-14); and law enforcement cooperation including joint investigations (Art. 19).

1.2 The RICO Act: the preeminent American instrument

For Tren de Aragua operations on American soil, the Racketeer Influenced and Corrupt Organizations Act

(RICO, 18 U.S.C. §§ 1961-1968) remains the most powerful prosecution instrument available. Its criminal enterprise theory — linking all participants in a racketeering pattern within a single indictment — allows capturing TdA's organizational dimension in a way that individual prosecutions cannot achieve.

The RICO case elements applied to TdA are: (1) "enterprise" — TdA as an identifiable criminal enterprise with structure and continuity; (2) "pattern of racketeering activity" — the documented pattern of extortion, trafficking, murder, drug trafficking, and money laundering; (3) "conduct" — each defendant's participation in conducting or managing the enterprise's affairs; and (4) "nexus" — the connection between individual conduct and the broader criminal enterprise. All TdA cases prosecuted in 2025 used RICO theory, validating its applicability to the organization's decentralized franchise model.

1.3 The FTO Designation: Full Legal Implications

The designation of the Tren de Aragua as a Foreign Terrorist Organization (FTO) under Section 219 of the Immigration and Nationality Act (published in the Federal Register on February 20, 2025) generates the following automatic legal consequences:

■ **Criminal liability for material support (18 U.S.C. § 2339B)**

Any person who knowingly provides "material support or resources" to TdA commits a federal offense with a maximum penalty of 20 years (or life imprisonment if conduct results in death). This includes providing lodging, transportation, funds, documentation, or services to TdA members.

- **U.S. entry prohibition**

  TdA members are inadmissible to the United States under the terrorism provisions of the Immigration and Nationality Act. The FTO designation facilitates inadmissibility determinations by CBP officers at ports of entry.

- **Asset freezing under American jurisdiction**

  The designation activates OFAC's authority to freeze any TdA assets under American jurisdiction and prohibit transactions with the organization or its designated members. This includes bank accounts, real estate, and financial assets.

II. Concrete Public Policy Recommendations

2.1 For the United States Congress

- **Recommendation 1: Authorize and fund the Venezuelan Criminal Records Verification Program**

  The greatest operational gap in the American response to TdA is the inability to verify the Venezuelan criminal backgrounds of individuals on American soil. Congress should authorize and fund the creation of an inter-agency program — in partnership with the Latino Institute for Security Efficiency and Venezuelan transitional authorities — to establish a Venezuelan criminal records verification mechanism. Details of this program are presented in Chapter Ten.

■ Recommendation 2: Dedicated funding for Venezuelan trafficking victim identification training

Federal agents, social workers, first responders, and immigration judges who interact with Venezuelan communities require specific training in TdA trafficking patterns, victim identification indicators, and T visa offer protocols. This training must be dedicated-funded and developed in collaboration with organizations with specific expertise in the Venezuelan community.

■ Recommendation 3: Legislation to address gota a gota and predatory lending in immigrant communities

The gota a gota operates in the regulatory vacuum of informal person-to-person lending. Specific legislation criminalizing predatory lending schemes with rates exceeding 100% annually as a federal offense, with aggravated penalties when targeted at immigrant communities, would close this gap and provide more direct prosecution tools.

2.2 For federal executive agencies

■ Recommendation 4: Establish a dedicated TdA intelligence unit with Venezuelan-expert component

Joint Task Force Vulcan is an important advance, but needs to be complemented by a specialized intelligence unit including professionals with deep knowledge of the Venezuelan judicial system, Venezuelan penitentiary records, and the organization's cultural and institutional codes. The Latino Institute for Security Efficiency, with its deep knowledge of the Venezuelan system and active federal vendor status, is positioned to contribute to this capability as a certified consultant.

■ Recommendation 5: Establish judicial cooperation protocols with transitional Venezuela

The political transition in Venezuela opens a unique window to establish the mutual legal assistance mechanisms (MLATs) that the Maduro regime systematically blocked for two decades. The Department of Justice, in coordination with the Department of State, must prioritize establishing cooperation agreements with Venezuelan transitional authorities to access criminal records, extradite identified TdA members, and share intelligence on the organization's networks.

■ Recommendation 6: Witness protection program extended to families in Venezuela

The most effective barrier to cooperation of Venezuelan witnesses — both victims and potential cooperators with organizational knowledge — is the credible threat against their families in Venezuela. The federal witness protection program (WITSEC) should be expanded, in collaboration with the Department of State and reliable Venezuelan organizations, to offer protection to witnesses' families remaining in Venezuela. Without this mechanism, cooperation from the most valuable witnesses will remain limited.

2.3 For state and local governments

■ Recommendation 7: Specialized Venezuelan community liaison units

Police departments in cities with high Venezuelan resident concentrations (New York, Miami, Houston, Aurora, Nashville, Chicago) should establish community liaison units specialized in the Venezuelan community. These units — ideally with bilingual, culturally competent officers — are the most effective instrument for building the community trust necessary for the information flow that makes TdA investigations possible.

■ Recommendation 8: Emergency funds for Venezuelan trafficking victim support

Trafficking victim support shelters and organizations in cities with high TdA presence are chronically over capacity. State and local governments should provide emergency funds specifically for Venezuelan trafficking victim care, including housing, medical care, culturally competent mental health services, and legal support for T visa and asylum applications.

III. The Latino Institute for Security Efficiency: The Value Proposition

Throughout this book, multiple gaps in the American institutional response to the Tren de Aragua have been referenced: the inability to verify Venezuelan backgrounds, the absence of Venezuelan cultural expertise in investigative units, the lack of reliable institutional intermediaries for cooperation with transitional Venezuela. These gaps are not individual deficiencies of any specific agency: they are the predictable result of the absence of an organization with the institutional profile, operational mandate, and deep knowledge of the Venezuelan system required to close them.

The Latino Institute for Security Efficiency (LISE) was founded to occupy precisely that space. With over fifteen years of prosecutorial experience in the Venezuelan judicial system, with access to institutional networks in Venezuela that no American agency possesses, and with active federal vendor status registered on SAM. gov, LISE is positioned to offer the capabilities that the gaps identified in this book require.

■ **Service 1: Intelligence consulting for federal agencies — Venezuelan system analysis**

Expert analysis of the Venezuelan judicial system, penitentiary records, TdA organizational patterns, and Venezuelan institutional contexts to support active investigations and develop prosecution strategies.

- **Service 2: Field agent training in TdA identification and Venezuelan context**

  Training programs for FBI, DEA, ICE, CBP, and local law enforcement agents on TdA's operational lexicon, member identification indicators, Venezuelan victim interview protocols, and the Venezuelan cultural and institutional context essential for effective work with this community.

- **Service 3: Venezuelan Criminal Records Verification Program (VCRVP)**

  The proposed program that leverages the Venezuelan transition to establish a Venezuelan criminal background verification mechanism for individuals under investigation or prosecution in the United States. Complete program details — its architecture, implementation phases, estimated costs, and effectiveness metrics — are presented in Chapter Ten.

IV. Summary: An Action Agenda for 2026

Maduro's capture on January 3, 2026 marked the beginning of a new phase in the history of the Tren de Aragua and in the American response to the threat it represents. The decisions made in the next 12 to 24 months — on cooperation with transitional Venezuela, on records access, on prosecution and victim support resources — will determine whether this historic moment translates into real and lasting impact on the organization, or whether the band simply adapts and continues.

This book has provided the map. The Latino Institute for Security Efficiency is available to accompany its implementation.

🔍 CONTACT AND CONSULTATION

To engage the services of the Latino Institute for Security Efficiency or to request a presentation before your agency, department, or legislative committee: Latino Institute for Security Efficiency (LISE) Executive Chairman: Rolnar Armando Sanabria Bernatte, J.D., LL.M., Ph.D. 7633 E 63rd Pl, Suite 300, Tulsa, OK 74133 Phone: (954) 326-1419 Email: info@latinoinstituteforsecurityefficiency.com Web: latinosecurity.com/en/ CAGE: 157Z2 | UEI: XQ1ELJLHYBR9 | SAM. gov active.

— END OF CHAPTER SEVEN —

CHAPTER EIGHT

The Regional and Global Response

Joint operations, terrorist designations, judicial victories, and lessons from the international front

Introductory Note: The Decisive Moment of the International Response

The year 2025 marked a historic inflection point in the global response to the Tren de Aragua. For the first time, the international community acted in concert to elevate TdA from a public order concern to a first-tier national security threat — with formal terrorism designations, multinational joint operations, historic judicial convictions, and the beginning of an unprecedented hemispheric coordination. This chapter documents that response, analyzes what worked, what failed, and what lessons must guide the next steps.

I. The Wave of Terrorist Designations: An Emerging Regional Consensus

1.1 The domino effect of 2025 designations

The designation of the Tren de Aragua as a Foreign Terrorist Organization by the United States on February 20, 2025 triggered a domino effect of designations across the region. Each designation is not merely symbolic: it activates specific legal tools — specialized military and judicial powers, international cooperation with a new legal foundation, and financial sanctions — that transform the operational capacity of law enforcement in adopting countries.

- **United States — February 20, 2025**

   Secretary of State Marco Rubio formally designated TdA as an FTO under 8 U.S.C. § 1189, published in the Federal Register (FR Doc. 2025-02873). Simultaneously, the Treasury Department activated OFAC sanctions freezing assets and prohibiting transactions with the organization. On March 14, President Trump invoked the 1798 Alien Enemies Act — the fourth invocation in American history — against TdA. Executive Order 14157, signed January 20, initiated the process culminating in the designation.

- **Argentina — February 2025**

   The Argentine Ministry of Security, under Minister Patricia Bullrich, classified TdA as a terrorist organization, incorporating it into the Public Registry of Persons and Entities Linked to Terrorist Acts — the same registry that includes al-Qaeda and individuals linked to Hezbollah and the AMIA bombing. This was the second hemispheric designation after the U.S. and enabled specialized judicial and intelligence powers. In May 2025, Argentine authorities arrested 12 alleged TdA members.

- **Ecuador — 2025**

  Ecuador designated TdA as a terrorist organization, enabling the use of military intelligence instruments in its pursuit. The Ecuadorian designation is particularly significant given that Ecuador is a critical transit country on the Andean Route to the United States.

- **Trinidad and Tobago — 2025**

  Trinidad and Tobago elevated TdA to terrorist status following a surge in TdA-linked illicit maritime activity in the southern Caribbean. The designation is operationally relevant because the island functions as a node of TdA's Caribbean human and drug trafficking route.

- **Texas — September 2024 (precursor to the federal wave)**

  Texas was the first U.S. state to designate TdA as a foreign terrorist organization, in September 2024, following documented increases in extortion and organized theft rings in San Antonio and Houston. This state designation preceded and pressured the February 2025 federal designation.

II. Joint Operations: What Has Been Achieved

2.1 Operation Crazy Train: The U.S. Sustained Campaign

"Operation Crazy Train" — an operation named with deliberate irony — is the most sustained and comprehensive prosecution campaign ever launched against the Tren de Aragua on American soil. Led by Homeland Security Investigations (HSI) New York, the operation has accumulated since its 2025 launch an unprecedented series of judicial achievements in the history of federal prosecution of Venezuelan criminal organizations.

- **Operation Crazy Train Timeline**

  April 2025: 27 TdA and Anti-Tren members charged with racketeering, drug trafficking, sex trafficking, arms trafficking, and murder-for-hire. Coordinated multi-state takedown. September 2025: Expanded superseding RICO indictment added murder, murder conspiracy, firearms use in violent crimes, and additional RICO violations against 10 members. December 2025: Federal grand jury indicts Niño Guerrero — the organization's leader — for racketeering conspiracy, material support to terrorists conspiracy, cocaine importation conspiracy, and machine gun possession. January 28, 2026: Superseding RICO indictment unsealed by HSI charging 19 members with 29 federal counts, including double murder, murder-for-hire, murder conspiracy, assault with dangerous weapons, armed robbery, kidnapping, sex trafficking, and firearms offenses. Additionally: 40 additional administrative arrests of members and associates; rescue of multiple trafficking victims; narcotics and illegal weapons seized.

HSI Acting Executive Associate Director John Condon described TdA in February 2026 as "one of the fastest-emerging transnational criminal organizations to encroach upon American soil" and declared that "no corners of the TdA and Anti-Tren enterprises are beyond the reach of justice." Operation Crazy Train remains active, with additional arrests expected as investigators continue mapping the organization's financial networks and communications infrastructure.

2.2 San Antonio Operations: The Neighborhood Model

On November 16, 2025, the Homeland Security Task Force executed a search warrant at an after-hours illicit nightclub in San Antonio, Texas, known to be frequented by TdA members. Result: over 150 arrests of illegal aliens, including 27 suspected TdA members, plus cocaine seizure, three firearms, and approximately $35,000 in cash. The operation involved 14 state, local, and federal agencies — including ICE, HSI, FBI — and constituted one of the largest-scale single-location TdA operations on American soil.

The San Antonio case illustrates a feature of TdA's operational model in American cities: the use of nighttime entertainment establishments — clubs, after-hours venues, bars — as operations, recruitment, and drug distribution centers. Entertainment venues with high Venezuelan concentration, especially those operating outside regular hours, are high-surveillance environments for TdA case units.

2.3 Chile: The Historic 560-Year Sentence

On March 6, 2025, one of the most significant judicial events in the history of regional combat against the Tren de Aragua occurred: a criminal court in the province of Arica, Chile, handed down sentences totaling approximately 560 years of imprisonment against 34 members of "Los Gallegos" — a TdA cell. The convicted, 31 Venezuelans and 3 Chileans, were found guilty of criminal association, drug and arms trafficking, kidnapping, and homicide, among other offenses. Chile's Public Prosecutor's Office described the proceeding as "historic" and as one of the "most relevant nationally in the fight against transnational organized crime."

Two weeks earlier, in Santiago, Chilean authorities dismantled the "Tren de Aragua Pirates" — another cell — through 21 raids in the metropolitan region, with 23 arrests. The Pirates' leader, Adrián Gómez alias "El Turco," had been arrested in the United States in December 2024; his lieutenants, Larry Álvarez alias "Changa" and Carlos Gómez alias "El Bobby," were arrested in Colombia. The transnational coordination that enabled the Pirates' dismantling — with the leader arrested in the U.S. and lieutenants in Colombia — is the cooperation model this book has argued is the only truly effective response to TdA.

2.4 Spain: TdA Arrives in Europe

On November 7, 2025, Spain's National Police executed Operation Interciti, dismantling the first confirmed Tren de Aragua cell on European soil. Thirteen detained across Barcelona, Madrid, Girona, A Coruña, and Valencia — operation coordinated by Spain's National Court (the tribunal responsible for terrorism, organized crime, and drug trafficking) with cooperation from the Colombian National Police and the European AMERIPOL-EL PACTO 2.0 project. Those arrested face charges of drug trafficking (including domestic production of "tusi" or pink cocaine), human trafficking, money laundering, and extortion. The cell had been active since at least 2023 in Barcelona and Madrid neighborhoods.

TdA's presence in Europe is not a surprise to criminologists who have followed the band's expansion: the organization follows the Venezuelan diaspora and the Venezuelan diaspora reaches Spain, Germany, the United Kingdom, France, and Italy. Operation Interciti confirms that the three-phase expansion pattern — exploratory, penetration, consolidation — the band perfected in Latin

America is replicating on the European continent. Spain, with approximately 500,000 Venezuelan residents, is TdA's natural entry point into Europe.

2.5 Colombia and Peru: battles on the regional front

Colombia remains the most active TdA operations laboratory outside Venezuela — and the battleground where institutional response has been most intense and simultaneously most contested. In February 2025, Colombian authorities arrested Jeison Lorca Salazar — considered the second most important TdA leader in Colombia — and Derwin Isaías Chávez Mora, one of the most internationally wanted by authorities and Interpol. In October 2025, the lawyer for "Larry Changa" — TdA second-in-command detained in Colombia — offered to provide information on the band's direct ties to the Maduro regime, including Diosdado Cabello and Defense Minister Vladimir Padrino López, in exchange for benefits under Colombia's "Paz Total" program.

In Peru, ICE assisted Peru's National Police in February 2025 in a joint operation that freed over 80 TdA trafficking victims in Lima — one of the largest documented rescue operations against the organization. Secure Free Society Initiative researchers documented that "within 72 hours, replacement cells reemerged," illustrating the franchise model's resilience against dismantling operations.

III. What We Learn from Successes and Failures

3.1 What works: lessons from successful operations

Comparative analysis of the most successful operations against TdA in 2025-2026 — Chile's sentencing, Spain's Operation Interciti, the U.S.'s Operation Crazy Train, Colombia's leadership capture — reveals a set of common characteristics that define effective strategies:

■ **1. Transnational coordination from the start**

The most significant successes — Chile's Pirates, Operation Interciti — resulted from multi-country coordination from early investigative stages, not as a later add-on. The correct model is not investigating locally and then notifying other countries: it is investigating jointly from the start, sharing intelligence in real time.

■ **2. Parallel financial investigation**

None of the most successful operations limited themselves to conventional criminal charges. All incorporated parallel financial investigation — money flow analysis, asset identification, MLAT requests for offshore assets — that dramatically increased impact on the organization's operational capacity.

■ 3. The criminal enterprise perspective (RICO/equivalents)

Operations that prosecuted TdA as a criminal enterprise — linking multiple defendants within the same racketeering pattern — achieved real organizational impact. Operations that prosecuted individuals in isolation generated arrest statistics without strategic impact. The RICO theory, applied rigorously, is the correct tool.

■ 4. The victim-centered approach as an investigative strategy

Operations that prioritized victim identification and protection — actively offering the T visa, guaranteeing non-prosecution, connecting with support services — obtained greater witness cooperation and built stronger cases. The victim-centered approach is not just the correct ethical position: it is the most effective investigative strategy.

3.2 What does not work: lessons from documented errors

⚠ ERROR 1: Mass identification without methodological basis

The March 2025 deportations resulted in the deportation of innocent individuals, litigation reaching the Supreme Court, and destruction of Venezuelan community trust. This error weakened American security.

⚠ ERROR 2: Mass pressure operations without structural follow-up

Mass arrest operations produce impressive statistics but limited organizational impact. The Secure Free Society Institute documented that within 72 hours of the Peru operation freeing 80 victims, replacement cells reemerged.

⚠ ERROR 3: Collective criminalization of the Venezuelan community

When security policy fails to distinguish between TdA criminals and legitimate Venezuelan migrants, it destroys community trust. Venezuelan residents who have suffered TdA activities are witnesses whose cooperation depends on being treated as victims, not suspects.

IV. The Future of the Response: Toward a Hemispheric Security Architecture

Maduro's capture on January 3, 2026 and Venezuela's political transition have created a historic window of opportunity to build the hemispheric security architecture that the Tren de Aragua threat requires. This architecture has five pillars:

■ Pillar 1: Real-time intelligence cooperation among affected countries

A real-time intelligence sharing system among the U.S., Colombia, Peru, Chile, Argentina, Spain, and transitional Venezuela — modeled on the Five Eyes system but specifically oriented toward Latin American transnational organized crime — would enable proactive identification of leadership and cell movements before they establish in new jurisdictions.

■ Pillar 2: Access to Venezuelan records — the LISE program

The Venezuelan Criminal Records Verification Program — detailed in Chapter Ten — is the most specific and urgent instrument available to close the information gap that has protected TdA members on American soil for two decades.

■ Pillar 3: Transnational joint investigation teams

Joint investigation teams (JITs) — in which investigators from multiple jurisdictions work together under a shared legal framework — are the operational instrument that best captures the transnational dimension of the threat. The European JIT model under the Eurojust framework offers directly applicable lessons for an American hemispheric framework.

■ Pillar 4: Sustained funding for victim support

An effective hemispheric response to TdA requires sustained funding for victim identification, care, and protection across all affected countries — not only in final destination countries but in transit countries where victims are recruited and exploited before reaching their final destination.

■ Pillar 5: Leveraging the Venezuelan transition

Venezuela's opening to international cooperation under the post-Maduro administration is potentially the factor that can most transform the hemispheric security landscape in relation to TdA. But that opening requires interlocutors who know the Venezuelan system from within — a capability examined in depth in Chapter Ten.

V. Summary: The Battle Map in 2026

The Tren de Aragua in 2026 is an organization under greater pressure than at any point in its history — but also more decentralized, more geographically diversified, and more operationally resilient than at any previous point. The tension between these two realities defines the security landscape in which this book is published.

The good news is that the tools to dismantle this organization exist: RICO theory, the FTO designation, MLATs, multinational cooperation, and — for the first time in two decades — the possibility of access to Venezuelan system records. The bad news is that these tools only work if used in a coordinated, sustained manner with the correct analytical precision. Chapter Ten proposes the most concrete instrument available to advance in that direction: the Venezuelan Criminal Records Verification Program.

— END OF CHAPTER EIGHT —

CHAPTER NINE

The Forensics of Terror:

Crime Scene, Victims, and Evidence in Tren de Aragua Cases.

The perspective of the prosecutor who processed organized crime cases in the system that incubated the Tren de Aragua

AUTHOR'S NOTE: This chapter represents a unique contribution to the criminological literature on the Tren de Aragua: the forensic criminology perspective of a Venezuelan prosecutor who processed organized crime cases, hostage-taking in detention centers, human trafficking, and strategic material smuggling within the same penal system that incubated this organization. The method described here is not theoretical — it comes from direct practice in Venezuelan criminal courts during the period of TdA's consolidation. The purpose is not to glorify the organization's crimes, but to provide federal agents, prosecutors, and forensic technicians with the methodological tools to investigate them effectively.

I. The Crime Scene in TdA-Related Cases

1.1 Anatomy of a Typical Crime Scene

Understanding what a Tren de Aragua crime scene looks like requires first understanding the organization's operational philosophy: the TdA does not commit crimes — it administers territories. Its acts of violence are, mostly, acts of criminal governance: messages to populations, executions of internal sentences, or demonstrations of force against rivals or authorities. This distinction is fundamental to the forensic investigator, because it determines the nature and disposition of physical evidence.

Unlike impulsive or reactive crimes, TdA crime scenes frequently exhibit characteristics of advanced planning and organized execution. These are not heat-of-passion homicides — they are operations. The investigator who arrives at a scene without understanding this distinction will misinterpret the evidence.

Distinctive physical characteristics

TdA-linked crime scenes exhibit recurring patterns documented across multiple jurisdictions:

- Absence of ballistic material: TdA instructs its members to collect shell casings. Nixon Perez, indicted in Colorado in 2024, was prosecuted precisely for collecting ballistic evidence from a crime scene before police arrived — a practice that reveals organizational training in scene contamination.

- Deliberate body disposition: In high-profile cases, the organization uses the disposal of the corpse as a message. The most documented case is that of Lieutenant Ronald Ojeda in Chile (February 2024), whose remains were found in a suitcase buried under concrete. This technique — "cementing" bodies — was also documented in the Los Gallegos cases in Arica, Chile, where 16 people were found buried under concrete slabs in clandestine graves.

- Crime scene relocation: TdA frequently executes in one location and moves the body to another. This creates two scenes — the primary (where the crime occurs) and the secondary (where the body appears) — and complicates the reconstruction of events. For the forensic investigator, identifying whether the scene is primary or secondary is the first critical step.

- Chemical cleaning of the primary scene: Documented in Chilean and Colombian cases, TdA uses bleach and other agents to contaminate surfaces at the primary scene before moving the body. This does not eliminate all biological evidence — luminol and alternative light source techniques remain effective — but significantly complicates collection.

- Multiple projectiles in different vectors: Unlike a simple execution (shot to the back of the head), TdA homicides frequently exhibit multiple impacts at different angles, indicating more than one shooter from different positions — a pattern consistent with the "carro" (operational cell) structure of the gang.

- Falsified police equipment: Documented in the Ojeda case in Chile, where captors dressed as police. The presence of badges, uniforms, or vehicles imitating authorities at the scene or in eyewitness accounts is a high-specificity TdA indicator.

Differences from other criminal organizations

Characteristic	Tren de Aragua	MS-13	Mexican Cartels
Visual signature	Absent or minimal. No consistent ritual signatures.	High. Ritual cuts, body positioning.	High. Dismemberment with written messages.
Communication language	Venezuelan prison lexicon. Emojis in digital.	English and Spanish with Salvadoran slang.	Mexican Spanish with regionalisms.
Primary target of violence	Territorial control and own victims (Venezuelan migrants).	Territorial control. Rivals and witnesses.	Drug trafficking. Rivals and the State.
Body disposal	Frequent relocation. Concrete burial documented.	Ritual positioning. Visible body	Dismemberment and public display frequent.

Characteristic	Tren de Aragua	MS-13	Mexican Cartels
		as a message.	
Digital evidence	WhatsApp/Telegram with coded emojis. Critical.	Facebook. Less digitally sophisticated.	Variable. High sophistication in larger groups.

II. Forensic Identification of TdA Victims

2.1 The Challenge: Victims Who Do Not Speak

The forensic identification of Tren de Aragua victims faces a unique challenge: most victims — especially those of sex trafficking — do not identify themselves as such. Fear, debt bondage, psychological control, and direct threats against their families in Venezuela create systematic silence that the forensic investigator cannot break through traditional methods. Physical evidence becomes, therefore, the only available language.

Ownership marks — the most specific evidence

The U.S. Department of State documented in its 2025 Trafficking in Persons Report on Colombia that the Tren de Aragua "allegedly marked women and girls behind their ears to prove ownership." This mark — consistently reported by multiple independent sources — is the highest-specificity physical indicator documented for TdA victimization. Unlike tattoos, which can be cultural and ambiguous, the mark behind the ear on a Venezuelan woman with other trafficking indicators has high diagnostic specificity.

For the forensic technician or first responder, the identification protocol must include, as a standard step in every Venezuelan female victim:

- Visual inspection behind both ears for burn marks, scars, or small tattoos applied without professional equipment.

- Photographic documentation of any irregular mark in that area before any medical procedure that might alter the evidence.

- Recording whether the victim reacts with disproportionate fear when examined in that specific area — a response consistent with trauma conditioning.

Indicators of sustained violence — the body as a case file

TdA trafficking victims frequently present a pattern of injuries that differs from the acute trauma associated with conventional violent crimes. The forensic investigator must look for evidence of chronic violence, not just recent injuries:

- Multiple scars in different stages of healing, consistent with repeated violence over an extended period. This differs from the acute trauma of a single event.

- Untreated old fractures — documented in trafficking victims who did not receive adequate medical care during their period of exploitation. X-rays reveal histories of violence that the victim does not verbally report.

- Genital injuries consistent with chronic forced sexual activity — critical medico-forensic evidence that must be documented with specialized protocols (SANE nurse where available).

- Chronic malnutrition and dehydration — not always externally visible, but documentable in blood analysis. Trafficking victims frequently live in conditions of controlled deprivation as an additional dominance mechanism.

III. Documented Cases — Forensic Methodology in Action

3.1 The Ojeda Case — When the Crime Scene Speaks for the System

The murder of Lieutenant Ronald Ojeda Moreno in Santiago, Chile, on February 21, 2024, represents the most complex and documented forensic criminology case linked to the Tren de Aragua to date. Its analysis illustrates both the criminal methodology of the organization and the forensic tools that allowed the case to be reconstructed.

Ojeda was kidnapped from his apartment by men dressed as police. The initial scene — his residence — presented characteristics of advanced planning: no signs of struggle, no ballistic evidence, no direct witnesses. The use of police uniforms as an entry method eliminated resistance and contaminated the perception of neighbors who might have observed the operation.

Ten days later, an anonymous call directed authorities to the body's location: buried under 4.5 feet of concrete, inside a suitcase. The secondary scene revealed significant logistical planning — the concrete required advance preparation, materials, and curing time, indicating that the disposal site was prepared before or during the kidnapping, not improvised.

The Chilean investigation reconstructed the case through: surveillance camera analysis, forensic analysis of WhatsApp conversations found on subsequently detained suspects linking the executors to the TdA's "Los Piratas" cell, cell signal triangulation tracking suspects' movements, and concrete analysis establishing the curing time and therefore the interment window. The conclusion — that the crime was ordered from Caracas by Diosdado Cabello and executed by the TdA — is an example of transnational case building that combines digital evidence, materials analysis, and international collaboration.

3.2 Los Gallegos in Arica — The Torture Chamber as Crime Scene

The Chilean police operation that dismantled the TdA's "Los Gallegos" cell in Cerro Chuño, Arica, revealed one of the most complex crime scenes documented in South America linked to this organization. The operation found: 80 kilograms of illicit substances, 18 automatic rifles and machine guns, over 1,000 rounds of ammunition, clandestine torture chambers, houses of prostitution using minors as victims, and clandestine burial sites where multiple victims were found buried alive under concrete slabs.

The forensic criminology of the torture chambers revealed systematic method — not an impulsive crime. The spatial arrangement, restraint elements, and cleaning techniques evidenced repeated use and established protocol. For the forensic investigator, these elements are critical because they distinguish instrumental violence (from TdA as a criminal enterprise) from reactive violence. The mega-trial that followed resulted, in March 2026, in convictions for 34 of 38 defendants, with cumulative sentences of 560 years — the largest judicial victory against TdA in the hemisphere to date.

IV. Chain of Custody: Venezuela vs. the United States

4.1 The American Standard

The American federal evidence handling system is built on two pillars: an unbroken chain of custody and verifiable authenticity. The Federal Rules of Evidence (FRE) establish that any physical evidence presented at trial must be able to trace its complete trajectory — from the crime scene to the courtroom — with documentation identifying who handled it, when, and under what conditions. The standard operationalized by NIST and the FBI requires: signed chain of custody forms at each transfer, tamper-evident packaging with numbered seals, storage in ISO/IEC 17025-accredited laboratories, systematic photographic and video documentation, individual labeling of each item, and digital traceability through evidence management systems.

4.2 The Venezuelan System — Gaps That Create Transnational Impunity

The Venezuelan evidence handling system, in theory, responds to the Organic Code of Criminal Procedure (COPP) and standards of the Scientific, Penal, and Criminal Investigations Corps (CICPC). The institutional collapse of the Venezuelan State has created systematic gaps that make it nearly impossible to use Venezuelan evidence in American federal proceedings.

As a prosecutor who worked directly with the CICPC during the years of TdA's consolidation, the author can document the following critical differences:

- Paper forms without digital backup: The CICPC used paper forms that were lost, deteriorated, or altered without possibility of subsequent verification. The American system has migrated to electronic traceability that generates automatic audit trails.

- Laboratories without international accreditation: Venezuelan forensic laboratories lack ISO/IEC 17025 accreditation, making their results challengeable before American courts under the Daubert standard (which requires recognized and reproducible scientific methodology).

- Systemic contamination: In Venezuelan detention centers where TdA operated autonomously, the custodians themselves were frequently members or collaborators of the organization. Evidence collected in those contexts carries a presumption of contamination that any competent defense will exploit.

- Broken chain due to institutional collapse: Complete Public Ministry files were destroyed, lost, or made inaccessible after the post-2016 institutional collapse. Evidence that could link TdA members to earlier crimes simply does not exist in usable form.

4.3 Impact on American Federal Proceedings

These gaps have concrete procedural consequences in federal TdA cases in the United States. SDNY prosecutors building RICO cases against TdA leaders face the challenge of demonstrating patterns of conduct that, mostly, occurred in Venezuela under a system that cannot certify the integrity of its own evidence. Solutions adopted include reliance on digital evidence, testimony over documentary evidence, and the Venezuelan Criminal Records Verification Program (VCRVP) detailed in Chapter Ten of this book.

V. Technical Recommendations for Agents and Prosecutors

5.1 Identification Protocol for FBI, DEA, and ICE Agents

LEVEL 1 — INITIAL IDENTIFICATION: Do not act based on physical appearance or tattoos in isolation. The cost of a misidentification — demonstrated in the incorrect CECOT deportations of 2025 — is legally devastating to the investigation. Require correlation of multiple indicators before documenting someone as a TdA member.

LEVEL 2 — BEHAVIORAL INDICATORS: Look for behavior and pattern, not appearance: use of Venezuelan prison lexicon (pran, carro, vacuna, multada, convive), evasive responses specific to the Venezuelan penitentiary system, ability to describe TdA internal structure without having been able to know it through public means, and documented associations with other individuals with confirmed connections.

LEVEL 3 — DIGITAL EVIDENCE: The phone is the case file. Obtain a judicial order for mobile device analysis. Prioritize: WhatsApp groups with organizational lexicon, payment history through remittance apps to Venezuela, emojis in communication patterns identified in federal indictments (🧱🔒🍬📦), and communications with Venezuelan numbers with +58 prefix.

LEVEL 4 — BACKGROUND VERIFICATION: Request Venezuelan background verification through available channels. INTERPOL maintains red notices for known TdA leaders. For mid and low-level organization members — where independent verification is more difficult — the Venezuelan Criminal Records Verification Program provides access to Venezuelan Public Ministry records not available in international databases.

LEVEL 5 — VICTIMS FIRST: In any operation with presumed trafficking victims, immediately separate victims from perpetrators. Do not use victims as interpreters. Provide access to certified Venezuelan interpreters. Apply FOSTA-SESTA and T Visa protocols from first contact. A victim who perceives she will be deported rather than protected will not cooperate — and the most valuable testimonial evidence in the case will be lost.

5.2 What Every American Forensic Technician Must Know About Venezuelan Methodology

The American forensic technician working TdA cases faces an epistemological challenge: the organization was formed in a system whose investigative method is radically different from the American one. Understanding those differences is not an academic exercise — it is operationally critical.

The TdA was formed, organized, and perfected inside a prison. This means its members were trained in an environment where observing routines, designing operations within controlled spaces, and evading surveillance were everyday survival skills. A TdA member with experience in Tocorón has practical knowledge of how institutional security systems work — and how to evade them.

The pranato system — where control is exercised through the provision of security, services, and "justice" within a territory — is the organizational model TdA exported from Venezuelan prisons to diaspora communities. When the FBI or DEA builds a network map of TdA in an American city, they should look for it not as a pyramidal organization but as a portable pranato system: Who provides "security" to the local Venezuelan community (and charges for it)? Who resolves internal disputes — who acts as "judge"? Who controls access to jobs, housing, or other scarce resources for migrants? The person in that central role is the local pran. Identifying them is identifying the cell.

VI. Conclusion: The Evidence the Venezuelan System Cannot Provide

This chapter has described methodologies, protocols, and analytical frameworks. But its most important conclusion is structural: the greatest forensic gap in the investigation of the Tren de Aragua is not technical — it is institutional. American investigators cannot access the evidence that exists in Venezuela, and evidence that arrives from Venezuela frequently cannot be certified for federal courts.

This gap is not closed by a better forensic camera, more sophisticated DNA analysis, or more rigorous chain of custody protocols on the American side. It is closed by access to Venezuelan penal system records — Public Ministry files, Tocorón penitentiary records, CICPC backgrounds — certified by someone who knows that system from the inside and can guarantee their authenticity before an American court.

That is exactly what the Latino Institute for Security Efficiency's Venezuelan Criminal Records Verification Program offers. Not as a theoretical promise — but as operational capacity grounded in direct institutional knowledge of the system, the TdA calls home.

Latino Institute for Security Efficiency |
info@latinoinstituteforsecurityefficiency.com | (954) 326-1419 |
latinosecurity.com/en/

CAGE: 157Z2 | UEI: XQ1ELJLHYBR9 | SAM. gov Active through
09/07/2026

— END OF CHAPTER NINE —

CHAPTER TEN

The Venezuelan Criminal Records Verification Program

The Latino Institute for Security Efficiency's proposal to close the information gap that has protected TdA

Author's Note: The Chapter This Book Exists to Write

All previous chapters have been, in their essence, preparation for this one. The analysis of transnational organized crime, the history of Venezuela's collapse, the anatomy of the Tren de Aragua, the horror of human trafficking, the criminal financial architecture, the available legal framework, the regional response underway — all that knowledge converges in one practical and urgent question: how do we close the information gap that has protected this organization on American soil for two decades?

The answer — the Venezuelan Criminal Records Verification Program — is this book's central proposal. It is not theory: it is a concrete operational mechanism, founded on fifteen years of prosecutorial experience in the Venezuelan system, backed by the Latino Institute for Security Efficiency's active federal vendor status, and calibrated to leverage the historic window that Venezuela's political transition has opened.

I. The Problem: The Information Gap Nobody Has Been Able to Close

1.1 Why Venezuelan records are the central problem

Imagine an ICE agent detaining a Venezuelan national during a TdA operation. The individual has no criminal record in the United States. Has no records in FBI databases accessible to the agent. Claims not to be a TdA member. Without Venezuelan records — without access to the Venezuelan Public Ministry's files, without access to Tocorón's penitentiary system records, without access to Venezuelan state criminal intelligence — the agent faces an affiliation determination decision with incomplete information. That gap, reproduced thousands of times per year, is what has allowed documented TdA members to operate on American soil while evading identification.

This is not a hypothesis: it is the operational reality documented in all previous chapters. The January 3, 2026 indictment against Maduro explicitly identified the Venezuelan state's refusal to cooperate with international agencies as an element of the criminal scheme. The failure of the March 2025 deportations — in which innocent individuals were sent to CECOT because there was no reliable way to verify their Venezuelan backgrounds — illustrates the human and legal consequences of this gap.

1.2 The historic opportunity of 2026

Maduro's capture on January 3, 2026, and the emergence of a transitional administration in Venezuela have created, for the first time in two decades, the genuine possibility of establishing cooperation mechanisms for access to records that the previous regime had systematically blocked. The Rodríguez government, under simultaneous pressure from the international community and American economic sanctions, has shown initial signals of cooperative willingness that did not exist under Maduro.

This window will not remain open indefinitely. The history of political transitions in countries with deeply rooted criminal structures shows that criminal interests frequently manage to capture new institutions before reform consolidates. The time to act is now.

II. The Venezuelan Criminal Records Verification Program (VCRVP)

2.1 Program overview

The Venezuelan Criminal Records Verification Program (VCRVP) is the operational instrument designed to close the information gap that has protected the Tren de Aragua on American soil. The program has three main components:

■ **Component 1: Access and verification of Venezuelan Public Ministry records**

Venezuela's Public Ministry maintains records of all criminal investigations, charges, and convictions processed by the Venezuelan judicial system. These records include information on individuals prosecuted in Venezuela for TdA-related offenses, on judicially established links between individuals and the organization, and on criminal backgrounds of any type. Access to these records, through a cooperation mechanism between Venezuela's transitional Public Ministry and LISE as an intermediary with verified federal status, would allow American agencies to verify the backgrounds of individuals under investigation or prosecution with a level of certainty currently unattainable.

■ **Component 2: Verification of Venezuelan penitentiary system records**

Venezuelan penitentiary records — especially those from the Aragua Penitentiary Center (Tocorón) and other prisons where TdA merged its presence — document who was incarcerated at those facilities, during which periods, and what activities were documented during their incarceration. An individual with an incarceration record at Tocorón during the TdA control period (2013-2023) is an individual with a verifiable nexus to the organization that no other information source available in the U.S. can establish.

■ Component 3: Venezuelan contextual intelligence analysis

Beyond formal records, the VCRVP incorporates contextual intelligence analysis: the deep knowledge of actors, networks, patterns, and codes of the Venezuelan criminal system that no formal database can capture but that a professional with fifteen years of prosecutorial experience in that system can provide. This component is the most difficult to formalize but the most valuable in terms of its capacity to inform investigative decisions in real time.

2.2 The three implementation phases

The program is implemented in three progressive phases, each building on the previous one and expanding the system's reach and capacity:

● Phase 1 (0-6 months): Establishment of bilateral cooperation mechanism

Objective: Establish formal agreements with Venezuelan transitional authorities enabling initial access to Public Ministry and penitentiary system records. Activities: Negotiation and signature of a cooperation agreement between LISE and Venezuela's transitional Public Ministry; definition of protocols for requesting, verifying, and transmitting information; training of Venezuelan personnel in format and authenticity requirements for judicial use in the U.S.; pilot with a limited set of high-value verification requests. Deliverables: Operational verification protocol; pilot effectiveness report; adjustment recommendations based on the pilot.

- **Phase 2 (6-18 months): Scaling and integration with federal systems**

    Objective: Scale the verification program to full operational capacity and integrate its outputs with the investigative systems of federal agencies working TdA cases. Activities: Expansion of verification capacity to multiple record categories; integration of VCRVP outputs with ICE, FBI, DEA, and HSI case management systems; training of federal agents in the correct interpretation and use of verified information; establishment of response times for urgent requests (maximum 72 hours for high-priority requests). Deliverables: Operational verification system at full scale; integration agreements with federal agencies; usage and effectiveness statistics for the period.

- **Phase 3 (18-36 months): Regional expansion and sustainability**

    Objective: Expand the verification mechanism to include information from other countries where TdA operates and has institutional records, and establish the program's long-term sustainability. Activities: Extension of cooperation agreements to Colombia, Peru, and Chile — the countries with the largest volume of TdA records outside Venezuela; development of a sustained financing model combining federal contracts with contributions from beneficiary countries; Congressional proposal for funding as a dedicated budget line. Deliverables: Multi-jurisdictional regional verification system; sustained financing model; period impact report.

III. The LISE Differentiator: Why Only We Can Do This

Several organizations and think tanks have identified the Venezuelan records gap as a problem. None has the capacity to close it that the Latino Institute for Security Efficiency possesses. That distinction is not modesty: it is a factual description of the unique capabilities that converge in LISE and that no other actor — governmental or private — replicates:

■ 1. Fifteen years of experience in the Venezuelan judicial system

Rolnar Armando Sanabria Bernatte, LISE's Executive Chairman, served as a prosecutor in Venezuela's Public Ministry for over fifteen years. In that period he prosecuted thousands of criminal cases, including cases related to the Venezuelan penitentiary system and criminal organizations that preceded and nurtured the Tren de Aragua. That knowledge — of the processes, actors, formats, codes, and institutional culture of the Venezuelan system — cannot be acquired through external consulting or document analysis. It is lived experience.

■ 2. Academic credentials in International Law and Criminology

Rolnar Sanabria Bernatte holds a J.D. (equivalent to an American law degree, accredited by Morningside Evaluations), an LL.M. (equivalent to a Master of Laws), and a Ph.D. in International Public Law from the Universidad Latinoamericana y del Caribe (2024), equivalent to a Doctor of Philosophy in Human Rights per Morningside evaluation. He is also a specialist in Criminal Law and International Human Rights Law. These credentials position LISE not as a generic service provider but as an academic and professional authority in the field.

■ 3. Institutional networks in Venezuela that no American agency possesses

Rolnar Sanabria Bernatte's fifteen years of prosecutorial experience in the Venezuelan system have built a network of professional relationships with prosecutors, judges, Public Ministry officials, penitentiary system directors, and Venezuelan criminal analysts. These relationships — the product of years of joint work on real cases — are the most difficult asset to replicate and the most valuable for accessing records and interpreting Venezuelan information.

■ 4. Active federal vendor status with current SAM. gov registration

LISE is registered on SAM. gov as an active federal vendor, with CAGE Number 157Z2 and UEI XQ1ELJLHYBR9, with active registration through 09/07/2026. This status allows LISE to contract directly with federal agencies including DOJ, DHS, FBI, DEA, and the DHS Office of Intelligence and Analysis, without the certification process delays that organizations without this status would face. LISE has previously received correspondence from the DOJ Criminal Division recognizing it as a potential vendor for services in its area of expertise.

IV. The Federal Business Case: Why Government Should Invest in the VCRVP

For officials and legislators evaluating the VCRVP as a federal spending proposal, the question is not whether the problem exists — previous chapters have established that clearly — but whether the proposed solution is worth its cost. The answer requires quantifying both the cost of the problem and the value of the solution.

■ The cost of the problem: the Venezuelan records gap in numbers

The failure of the March 2025 deportations — in which the records gap directly contributed to the deportation of innocents — generated: federal litigation that reached the Supreme Court; a costly and diplomatically sensitive prisoner exchange with Venezuela to repatriate CECOT deportees; damage to the relationship with El Salvador over the CECOT process; destruction of Venezuelan community trust in American cities with high TdA presence; and judicial invalidation of the Alien Enemies

Act as a rapid deportation instrument (September 2, 2025 ruling). The direct financial cost of that sequence — in litigation, diplomacy, and operations — exceeds any realistic VCRVP budget.

■ The value of the solution: the VCRVP in terms of return on investment

Each successful verification establishing TdA affiliation of an individual under investigation increases: the strength of the federal indictment and probability of conviction; the legal justification for preventive detention measures; RICO's capacity to connect the individual to the broader criminal enterprise; and the validity of immigration inadmissibility determinations that can withstand judicial review. Each verification establishing the absence of Venezuelan backgrounds in an individual under investigation prevents: the deportation of an innocent person (with all its associated legal and humanitarian costs); the alienation of a potentially valuable witness; and the destruction of the community trust that is the most valuable investigative asset available.

V. Immediate Recommendations: What Can Be Done Today

Without waiting for the full implementation of the VCRVP, there are concrete actions that federal agencies, Congress, and state governments can take today to begin closing the information gap and improving the effectiveness of the Tren de Aragua response:

■ **For DOJ and DHS today**

Engage the Latino Institute for Security Efficiency for an initial consulting phase that maps available Venezuelan records, establishes contacts with Venezuelan transitional authorities, and identifies the highest-priority TdA individuals whose Venezuelan backgrounds must be verified as a first priority. Incorporate LISE as a Venezuelan intelligence consultant in Joint Task Force Vulcan and Operation Crazy Train. Establish a Venezuelan background verification request protocol for all individuals charged in TdA cases within 60 days.

■ **For Congress today**

Convene a Homeland Security or Appropriations Committee hearing on the Venezuelan records gap as a specific security challenge, with the LISE Director participating as an expert witness. Include in the next Intelligence Authorization Act cycle a specific provision mandating pursuit of access to Venezuelan criminal records as an intelligence cooperation priority. Include in the FY2027 federal budget a funding line for the Venezuelan Criminal Records Verification Program.

■ **For state governments today**

States with the largest Venezuelan communities — New York, Florida, Texas, Colorado — should directly contact the Latino Institute for Security Efficiency to explore consulting agreements that improve their local law enforcement identification capacity. The cost of a state consulting agreement is marginal compared to the cost of failed investigations, litigation from misidentification, and community trust damage.

VI. Conclusion: One Book, One Proposal, One Window of Opportunity

This book began with a reality that only a former Venezuelan prosecutor can articulate with the authority of having lived it from the inside: Venezuela's state collapse was not an accident. It was the product of deliberate decisions made by concrete actors, over decades, that destroyed the institutions meant to protect Venezuelan society. The Tren de Aragua was the most devastating product of that process.

That collapse exported a monster to the world. The monster is in Chile, Colombia, Peru, Spain, forty-six states of the United States. It is in Nashville motels, in Aurora apartment buildings, in the Bronx, in the Darién Gap trochas. It is in the fake Instagram ads that promise work to desperate women. It is in the destroyed dreams of millions of Venezuelans who only wanted a better life.

Maduro's capture on January 3, 2026, opened a window. Venezuela's political transition, fragile and still uncertain, offers for the first time in two decades the possibility of accessing the archives that document who built this monster, who operated it, and who continues doing so from our own cities.

This window will not remain open indefinitely. History teaches us that political transitions in countries with deep criminal structures are fragile and reversible. The time to act is now.

The Latino Institute for Security Efficiency exists to help ensure that time is not wasted. Fifteen years of prosecutorial experience in the system that incubated the Tren de Aragua. A team of professionals with the knowledge, networks, and mandate to transform that knowledge into security for American communities. Active federal status ready for immediate contracting.

The book ends here. The work is just beginning.

🔍 CONTACT FOR FEDERAL CONTRACTS AND CONSULTING

Latino Institute for Security Efficiency Executive Chairman: Rolnar Armando Sanabria Bernatte, J.D., LL.M., Ph.D. 7633 E 63rd Pl, Suite 300, Tulsa, Oklahoma 74133-1202 Phone: (954) 326-1419 Email: info@latinoinstituteforsecurityefficiency.com Website: latinosecurity.com/en/ CAGE Number: 157Z2 UEI:

XQ1ELJLHYBR9 SAM.gov: Active through 09/07/2026
"The difference between knowledge and security is action.
Contact us today."

— END OF CHAPTER TEN —

Glossary of Key Terms

The following glossary defines the most relevant terms used in this book, with particular emphasis on the Tren de Aragua's operational lexicon, applicable American legal terms, and fundamental criminological concepts.

Anti-Tren:

Splinter faction of the Tren de Aragua, composed primarily of former members who left the original organization. Operates mainly in New York and northeastern U.S. cities, replicating TdA methodologies including sex trafficking of Venezuelan women. Indicted in the SDNY in April 2025 and January 2026.

Carro:

Minimum operational cell of the Tren de Aragua, composed of between three and fifteen individuals specialized in a specific criminal activity. Functional equivalent of a "unit" in military terminology. Carros operate with considerable tactical autonomy within the tren's organizational framework.

Causa (La Causa):

Internal system of periodic dues paid by members and inmates to the superior hierarchy. At Tocorón prison, generated estimated revenues of $3.5 million annually.

Convive:

Tren de Aragua member who has completed the formal initiation process and holds full status within the structure. Functional equivalent of a "made man" in the Sicilian Italian Mafia.

Coyote:

Facilitator for the transport of people — migrants or trafficking victims — across international borders. In the TdA context, coyotes are frequently contracted band members or contractors under its direction.

FTO (Foreign Terrorist Organization):

Formal designation by the U.S. Secretary of State under Section 219 of the Immigration and Nationality Act (8 U.S.C. § 1189). TdA was designated FTO on February 20, 2025. The designation activates criminal liability for material support (18 U.S.C. § 2339B), U.S. entry prohibition, and freezing of assets under American jurisdiction.

Criminal Governance:

Phenomenon by which criminal organizations substitute for legitimate state authority in territorial control, dispute resolution, coercive security provision, and resource extraction from the population. TdA developed criminal governance first in the Venezuelan penitentiary system and then in neighborhoods, border zones, and diaspora communities.

Gota a gota:

Usurious loan system with interest rates ranging from 20% to 100% monthly, with frequent payments. The name describes payments falling "drop by drop" on the borrower. Financial control instrument that converts borrowers into permanent debtors. Federal offense under 18 U.S.C. §§ 891-894.

Jackpotting:

Sophisticated cybercrime technique using malicious hardware or software to cause ATMs to dispense cash without authorization. TdA was indicted in Nebraska in 2025 for nationwide bank and ATM theft using this technique.

LISE (Latino Institute for Security Efficiency):

Federal consulting organization based in Tulsa, Oklahoma, specializing in transnational organized crime, border security, and criminal intelligence. CAGE: 157Z2 | UEI: XQ1ELJLHYBR9 | SAM. gov active through 09/07/2026.

Limpiar:

In TdA's internal lexicon, to execute a person by organizational order. May refer to disloyal members, witnesses, resistant victims, or rivals. In intercepted communications, "limpiar" or "hacer la limpieza" is coded language for ordering or confirming a murder.

MLAT (Mutual Legal Assistance Treaty):

Mechanism by which the United States requests or provides judicial help to other countries, including access to evidence, testimony, and records for American judicial proceedings. Fundamental instrument for transnational cooperation in TdA cases.

Multada:

TdA's internal term for sexual exploitation victims. From the Spanish "multa" (fine) — indicates the victim "must pay" the organization for transport or accommodation debts. High-value terminological indicator in intercepted communications. Documented in the SDNY indictment against Niño Guerrero (December 2025).

Niño Guerrero:

Alias of Héctor Rusthenford Guerrero Flores, supreme leader of the Tren de Aragua from its origins at Tocorón prison. Indicted in the SDNY in December 2025 for racketeering conspiracy, material support to terrorists, cocaine importation conspiracy, and machine gun possession. Fugitive with FBI reward exceeding $25 million. Whereabouts unknown at time of publication.

Operation Crazy Train:

Investigation and prosecution campaign led by HSI New York against the Tren de Aragua on American soil. Started in 2025, has resulted in RICO indictments against dozens of members, including the January 28, 2026 superseding RICO indictment with 19 defendants and 29 counts.

Pagadiario:

Daily-rate lodging low-cost, used by TdA as a victim recruitment point in Colombia and other transit countries. Victims accumulate daily debts for lodging and food that are then used as a control mechanism.

Plaza:

Territorial control zone where TdA has established stable criminal operations. The "plaza" concept replicated at the street level the territorial control system the band originally developed within the Venezuelan penitentiary system.

Pran:

De facto leader of a Venezuelan prison cell block or facility. Acronym popularized as "Preso Rematado Asesino Nato" (natural-born killer prisoner). Maximum authority in the pranato system. Héctor Guerrero Flores was the supreme pran of Tocorón.

Pranato:

Informal criminal governance system that ceded control of Venezuelan prisons to the most powerful inmate leaders — the pranes — in exchange for maintaining basic order. Institutionalized under Ministers Tareck El Aissami (2008-2012) and Iris Varela (2011-).

RICO (Racketeer Influenced and Corrupt Organizations Act):

American federal law (18 U.S.C. §§ 1961-1968) enabling the prosecution of criminal organizations as enterprises through demonstration of a pattern of racketeering activity. Primary instrument for TdA prosecution on American soil. Maximum penalty: 20 years per predicate act, plus criminal enterprise asset forfeiture.

SAR (Suspicious Activity Report):

Report filed by financial institutions with FinCEN when they detect transactions that may involve money laundering or other criminal activities. Key instrument in TdA financial investigation.

Sicariato:

Contract killing service. TdA revenue source and organizational control mechanism. Documented prices: $3,000-$50,000 per execution, depending on target profile and operation complexity.

Tren:

Mid-level organizational unit of TdA — a set of carros under shared leadership with assigned territory and criminal portfolio. The "tren-carro" structure is the band's fundamental organizational unit.

Trocha:

Informal unofficial border crossing used for irregular migration. Trochas are TdA's primary logistics routes for moving people, weapons, and drugs across Venezuelan and Latin American borders.

TVPA (Trafficking Victims Protection Act):

22 U.S.C. § 7101 et seq. Primary federal legal framework for human trafficking prosecution and victim protection. Establishes the T visa allowing cooperating victims to remain in the U.S. during investigation and prosecution.

Vacuna:

Periodic extortion payment demanded by TdA from businesses, residents, and other individuals in controlled territory. Analogous to the "Pizzo" of the Italian Cosa Nostra. The term reflects the "protection" offered against the very violence the organization threatens.

T Visa:

Non-immigrant visa available to trafficking victims who cooperate with authorities in investigation and prosecution. Allows staying in the U.S. for up to four years. Critical investigative instrument and chronically underutilized in TdA cases.

Bibliography and References

Legal and Government Documents

U.S. Department of Justice, Southern District of New York. United States v. Héctor Rusthenford Guerrero Flores et al. Superseding Indictment (unsealed December 18, 2025). RICO Conspiracy, Material Support to Terrorists, Cocaine Importation Conspiracy.

U.S. Department of Justice, Southern District of New York. United States v. Nicolás Maduro Moros et al. Superseding Indictment (unsealed January 3, 2026). Narco-Terrorism Conspiracy, Cocaine Importation Conspiracy.

U.S. Department of State. Federal Register, FR Doc. 2025-02873. Foreign Terrorist Organization Designations of Tren de Aragua et al. (February 20, 2025).

The White House. Executive Order 14157: Designating Cartels and Other Organizations as Foreign Terrorist Organizations and Specially Designated Global Terrorists (January 20, 2025).

The White House. Proclamation 10903: Invocation of the Alien Enemies Act Regarding the Invasion of the United States by Tren De Aragua (March 14, 2025).

U.S. Department of the Treasury, OFAC. Designation of Tren de Aragua as a Significant Transnational Criminal Organization (July 11, 2024). Press Release JY2459.

U.S. Department of Justice. Justice Department Highlights Nationwide Crackdown on Tren de Aragua (December 18, 2025).

U.S. Immigration and Customs Enforcement (ICE). HSI's Operation Crazy Train Continues to Dismantle Tren de Aragua (February 24, 2026).

U.S. Department of State. 2025 Trafficking in Persons Report — Colombia. Washington, D.C.: U.S. Department of State, 2025.

United Nations. United Nations Convention against Transnational Organized Crime and its Protocols (Palermo Convention). New York: United Nations, 2000.

UNODC. University Module Series E4J: Organized Crime. Vienna: United Nations Office on Drugs and Crime, 2024.

Academic Research and Specialized Reports

Erazo-Patiño, L., Laverde-Rodríguez, C.A. & Devia-Acevedo, E.D. (2025). Narratives and criminal diversification of transnational multicrime: the case of The Tren de Aragua en TikTok. Revista Criminalidad, 67(1), 13-24.

Dalby, Chris. (2024). *Tren de Aragua: The Guide to America's Growing Criminal Threat*. World of Crime.

James, Kane. (2024). *Tren de Aragua: From Prison Gang to Transnational Terror*. Independently Published.

Rísquez, Ronna. (2023). *El Tren de Aragua: La banda que revolucionó el crimen organizado en América Latina*. Editorial Planeta.

Sampó, C. & Troncoso, V. (2024). El Tren de Aragua: la transnacionalización del crimen organizado a través del tráfico de migrantes. Análisis político, 108. Bogotá.

Secure Free Society Institute. (December 2025). Weaponized Chaos: The Rise of Tren de Aragua as Venezuela's Proxy Force, 2014-2025.

Zeballos, P. & Farah, D. (2025). Tren de Aragua. El caso de Chile y repercusiones regionales: expansión, estructura y metodología. IBI Consultants / Fundación Taeda. Chile.

Human Rights Foundation. (April 2025). Venezuela's Maduro Continues to Use Tren de Aragua for Transnational Repression, Kidnapping, Assassination. New York: HRF.

Sanabria Bernatte, R.A. (2025). Patrones y tendencias que caracterizan el desplazamiento transnacional de la banda criminal "Tren de Aragua". Research Thesis, Criminal Law Specialist. San Cristóbal: Universidad Católica del Táchira.

Heritage Foundation. (2024). Derailing the Tren de Aragua. Washington, D.C.: Heritage Foundation.

InSight Crime. (August 2025). Tren de Aragua — Comprehensive Report. Washington, D.C.: InSight Crime.

Varese, F. (2011). Mafias on the Move: How Organized Crime Conquers New Territories. Princeton: Princeton University Press.

Paoli, L. (2002). The paradoxes of organized crime. Global Crime. DOI: 10.1080/17440570220000017814.

Journalistic and Media Sources

Lawfare Media. (January 7, 2026). Justice Department Unseals Superseding Indictment in Maduro Case.

JURIST. (January 5, 2026). The Charges Against Nicolás Maduro: What the Indictment Alleges.

NPR. (January 3, 2026). Venezuela's Nicolás Maduro and his wife face criminal charges in the United States.

Diálogo Américas. (April 2025). Latin America, Bent on Derailing the Tren de Aragua.

Diálogo Américas. (February 2026). Tren de Aragua's Global Leap: From Prison Gang to Transnational Threat.

Colombia One. (November 2025). Tren de Aragua Cell Dismantled in Spain; 13 Arrested.

West Hawaii Today. (December 2025). U.S. indicts alleged Tren de Aragua boss on murder, drug- and sex-trafficking charges.

Institutional Credentials & Expert Source Certifications

Office of the United Nations High Commissioner for Human Rights (OHCHR). (2018). Official Certification of Rolnar Armando Sanabria Bernatte as an Expert Source of Information for the United Nations Comprehensive Report on the Human Rights Situation in Venezuela (UN Resolution A/HRC/39/L.1/Rev.1). Geneva, Switzerland.

International Association for Identification (IAI). (2025). Official Educational Presentation: "Poster Presentation: Deconstructing Transnational Criminal Networks." 109th International Educational Conference. Approved by Domingo Villareal, Chairman of the Board, and Aldo Mattei, President. Orlando, Florida.

IAI Colombia Division & Policía Nacional de Colombia. (2025). International Expert Speaker Recognition: "Methodology for the Investigation of Transnational Criminal Threats" (Metodología para la Investigación de Amenazas Criminales Transnacionales). IV Congreso Internacional Forense, Escuela de Policía Carlos E. Restrepo. Certified by Jelmy Maritza Ballén García, President (E), and Cesar Augusto Hernández Rodríguez, Director of Training. Medellín, Colombia

Appendix A: Complete Timeline 1999-2026

1999 New Venezuelan Constitution — beginning of Chavista institutional Cappadocian.

2008-2012 Tareck El Aissami as Interior Minister — institutionalization of the pranato system.

2011 El Rodeo Riots — creation of the Ministry of Penitentiary Services — formalization of pranato.

2012-2017 El Aissami as Governor of Aragua — permissive environment for Tocorón.

2013 Niño Guerrero returns to Tocorón. Organized TdA expansion begins.

2015-2019 Great Venezuelan diaspora. TdA follows migration routes. Transnational expansion.

2017 El Aissami named Vice President. U.S. Treasury sanctions him as SDNTK.

2020 First U.S. federal indictment against Maduro. Initial reward: $15M.

February 2024 Murder of Ronald Ojeda in Santiago, Chile — by TdA members.

September 2023 Tocorón raid with 11,000 soldiers. Leadership escapes. Zoo, pools, arsenal found.

July 2024 OFAC designates TdA as Significant Transnational Criminal Organization.

September 2024 Texas designates TdA as terrorist organization (first U.S. state).

January 2025 Trump signs EO 14157 ordering terrorist designations.

February 2025 Secretary Rubio formally designates TdA as FTO. Argentina follows.

March 2025 Alien Enemies Act invoked. 238 Venezuelans deported to CECOT.

April 2025 27 TdA and Anti-Tren members indicted in SDNY — Operation Crazy Train.

June 2025 OFAC sanctions Giovanni Mosquera. FBI reward: $3 million.

July 2025 252 Venezuelans return from CECOT to Venezuela — prisoner exchange.

July 2025 OFAC sanctions Niño Guerrero. FBI reward: $25+ million.

September 2025 Appeals court: Alien Enemies Act does not apply to TdA.

November 2025 Spain dismantles first TdA cell in Europe — Operation Interciti. 13 arrested.

November 2025 DHS: San Antonio operation — 150 arrests, 27 TdA members.

December 2025 Federal grand jury indicts Niño Guerrero in SDNY — RICO + material support to terrorists.

January 3, 2026 Operation Absolute Resolve — Capture of Maduro and Cilia Flores in Caracas.

January 3, 2026 SDNY unseals superseding indictment: Maduro, Flores, Cabello, Maduro Guerra, and Niño Guerrero as co-defendants.

January 5, 2026 Maduro and Flores plead not guilty before Judge Hellerstein in Manhattan.

January 28, 2026 Operation Crazy Train superseding RICO indictment: 19 defendants, 29 counts.

March 2026 Chile: 560-year sentences for 34 members of Los Gallegos (TdA cell) in Arica.

Appendix B: Organizations, Designations, and Legal Frameworks

OFAC: Office of Foreign Assets Control — U.S. Treasury Department — Financial sanctions against TdA and its leaders

FinCEN: Financial Crimes Enforcement Network — SARs and Geographic Targeting Orders for laundering

SDNY: Southern District of New York — Primary federal jurisdiction for TdA cases

HSI: Homeland Security Investigations (ICE) — Operation Crazy Train and field operations

JTFV: Joint Task Force Vulcan — DOJ multi-agency coordination against TdA

INTERPOL: International Criminal Police Organization — Red notices for TdA leaders

UNODC: United Nations Office on Drugs and Crime — Palermo Convention framework

AMERIPOL: Organization of American Police Forces — Hemispheric police cooperation

Appendix C: Resources for Victims and First Responders

NATIONAL HUMAN TRAFFICKING HOTLINE

Phone: 1-888-373-7888 | Text: "HELP" to 233733 | Available 24/7, multiple languages

NATIONAL DOMESTIC VIOLENCE HOTLINE

1-800-799-7233 | 1-800-787-3224 (TTY) | thehotline.org

NATIONAL CENTER FOR MISSING AND EXPLOITED CHILDREN

1-800-843-5678 | missingkids.org

To report TdA activity to federal authorities:

FBI Tips: tips.fbi.gov | ICE Tips: 1-866-347-2423 | DEA Tips: 1-800-882-9539

Appendix D: Contact and Services — Latino Institute for Security Efficiency

Latino Institute for Security Efficiency

CAGE: 157Z2 | UEI: XQ1ELJLHYBR9 | SAM. gov active through 09/07/2026

Executive Chairman: Rolnar Armando Sanabria Bernatte, J.D., LL.M., Ph.D.

7633 E 63rd Pl, Suite 300, Tulsa, Oklahoma 74133-1202

Phone: (954) 326-1419

Email: info@latinoinstituteforsecurityefficiency.com

Website: latinosecurity.com/en/

Services available for federal and state contracting

- Intelligence consulting on the Tren de Aragua and Venezuelan organized crime for federal agencies (DOJ, DHS, FBI, DEA, HSI, CBP)

- Field agent training: TdA operational lexicon, member identification indicators, Venezuelan victim interview protocols

- Venezuelan Criminal Records Verification Program (VCRVP) — access to Venezuelan Public Ministry and penitentiary system records

- Venezuelan contextual intelligence analysis for cases under active investigation or prosecution

- Presentations before legislative committees, government agencies, and private security organizations

- Consulting for companies requiring background verification of employees of Venezuelan origin

www.ingramcontent.com/pod-product-compliance
Lightning Source LLC
Chambersburg PA
CBHW041309120726
48005CB00014B/1928